BUILDING TRUST WITH EMOTIONAL INTELLIGENCE

Learn non-verbal communication, workout your motivation, create a good team and be a good leader

_____By_____

Ashley Campbell

Table of Contents

Introduction 4

Chapter 1 29

Chapter 2 50

Chapter 3 71

Chapter 4 81

Chapter 5 104

Chapter 6 118

Chapter 7 125

Chapter 8 145

Conclusion 158

INTRODUCTION

Emotional intelligence is probably not a phrase you hear too much. It is still a fairly new field and many experts are still not in agreement as to what this type of intelligence truly measures.

However, its popularity as a study of human personality is growing all the time. In the sphere of human intelligence there are two very distinct areas; that of cognition and intelligence. However, the area of Emotional Intelligence does not fall within either cognition or intelligence.

Studies have been conducted as to how and how quickly a person can change between one emotional states to another. Of course, this is not an exact science. There are many differing parameters and variations depending on the person being studied and the circumstances involved. We all act differently to different situations; the emotional response will never be a constant. These variables are of course the major problem in determining how to accurately measure emotional intelligence.

There is no clear dividing line between intelligence and knowledge. Some state that emotional intelligence totally dynamic can be increased and decreased, will change with each person and with what that person is experiencing. Yet others claim the total opposite stating that people's emotions are constant and therefore are not affected by any situation. My personal opinion is that I tend to disagree with the latter.

Despite these conflicts there seems to be one constant belief, that our emotions are something that are developed over time. In other words we are not born with our emotions and develop them as we grow and learn. We can therefore say that emotional intelligence is our capacity as human beings to define our own emotions by the people, the circumstances and events we encounter, our environment.

We use our emotions to control how we react to situations and is therefore a major factor in determining our personality, who we are. The number of definitions as to what emotional intelligence really is, of course, far too many and complex for this short article however, what we can confirm is that there are two constants in all this. Firstly, the concept of what emotions are and secondly, understanding the context of emotions.

Be intelligent, follow the footprints of intelligent people, take their learning's and train under them so that you could also grab the wisdom they ac□uire. These are the stereotype statements made by our parents, relatives, senior citizen and even boss in the office.

It means being aware and intelligent in handling the situation is the key to debunk the formula of success. What kind of intelligence these guys are talking about? Are they talking about logical intelligence, which includes reasoning, detecting patterns, scientific investigations, decoding innovative and creative ideas, etc?

Almost 90% of the population possesses logical intelligence, spoon fended by school/ college and experience collected with seniors and society, then why do they fail in life. Stress, tension, poor health, failed relationship are their best buddies and with time they also lose self-esteem and confidence in life.

So, it is evident that logical intelligence can push your success graph to an extent, but saturate after a point. Is intelligence really the panacea for all your tensions and miseries? My answer is yes, intelligence appended with emotions and feelings. It is called emotional intelligence.

There are ☐uite a number of definitions for it. Most people will define this as an art whereby an individual is able to synchronize his mind and body acts through mind control acts; some define the subject as a high aura impulses which aid an individual react to situation. All these individuals are right; any individual who's attained emotional cleverness creates lots of advantages in his life. It is very important to understand a normal individual has a certain degree of emotional intelligence; however people can train their minds to attain higher levels of this art. There are ☐uite a number of informational sites which have detailed information on how people can train their minds to attain emotional intelligence, these informational sites are very important to individuals who may be interested in training their minds to attain emotional intelligence.

WHAT IS EMOTIONAL INTELLIGENCE

Emotional intelligence is the ability to become aware about the emotions, create and access the emotions and manage our emotional wealth to encourage our personal, professional and spiritual growth. The benefit is if you are completely aware about your emotions and control your actions and reactions, you can easily self-motivate and motivate everyone around, developing strong rapport and social skills with others and express compassion for others.

Twenty century displayed the substance of IQ (Intelligence Quotient), people character was judged on the basis of intelligent ☐uotient. In a layman language, the ability to become money spinner and accord every luxurious entity possible.

Various researches have suggested that it is a failed exercise. To lead a happy, prosperous and successful life emotional intelligence is re☐uired. Although intelligent ☐uotient is measured under certain parameters mental age and chronological age, but emotional intelligence has no such parameters and can be enhanced at any stage of life.

For anyone interested in attaining emotional intelligence then creating a right mental attitude before engaging these acts determines of one is actually going to be successful in the art. It is very important for individual to build up belief systems which are effective beneficial in delivering the kind of success they wish to achieve. One should also seek information on how they can manipulate   or   rather   take advantage of universal laws to affect the desired change. Contrary to what many believe, laws of attraction are very instrumental in shaping an individual personality. People who encourage wrong mental thoughts to crowd their minds more often than not have a very negative personality which hinders good overall lifestyles. It is very important for an individual to train their minds to be hopeful in any given situation as this is the essence of not only gaining emotional cleverness but also success in anything an individual does.

It is very important to understand that attaining self-development acts in any area of live is not a one day activity. One should always be consistent and persistent in any self-development act so as to achieve the desired success. The level for self-development success achievement will always be measured by efforts an individual is willing to put forth towards attaining what he or she desires.

let's take a look at some examples;

Two ladies, Sally and Freda, are to give presentations to some important clients. They have two weeks to prepare which they both consider time enough. Naturally, both are nervous, but Sally finds that every time she thinks about this presentation, she becomes more nervous still.

Unfortunately, she takes this as a sign that she's going to do a bad job of it. So straight away, her imagination has made up her mind for her. She knows it's going to be a shambles. She sets to and tries to prepare, but all the time she's working away, she feels this awful anxiety taking over.

This affects her sleeping and eating habits, and she finds she can't concentrate on anything. Try as she might, the closer the time comes, the more her mind turns to mush.

Finally, the day arrives, and while she's managed to come up with a presentation, she really isn't very happy with it. She starts speaking, but is visibly nervous. She finds she has to refer to her notes too often and then the worst happens. She discovers her notes are out of order.

For the rest of the time she wings it. She tries a couple of jokes, which don't even raise a smile. By the end of the presentation, she's a wreck.

Let's see how Freda's doing. Well, she's nervous too, but finds there's a tinge of excitement about the whole thing. She understands that her nervousness is natural and in any case, she needs some adrenaline to be at her best. To begin with, she reads up on her subject thoroughly before even starting to prepare.

Now having the subject firmly in her mind, she sets down and prepares. The closer she comes to the time, she feels certain nervousness, but realizes that it's the adrenaline. She thinks up some pretty good jokes, and then rehearses. By the time the big day arrives, she feels nervous for the first couple of minutes and then hits her stride.

Her first couple of jokes brings smiles, and a couple more, outright laughter. Buoyed by this, she finishes her talk on a wave of success. Freda also used self-hypnosis techniques to both relax her and build her confidence. In this way, she's able to gear her unconscious mind to success.

There are some who say that Emotional Intelligence skills can't be learned; that you're born with them or not. They're wrong. These skills can be learned, as I'm sure is fairly obvious in the foregoing examples.

There are several things that constitute the broad spectrum of emotional intelligence. When you set out to find out what it is, there are a few things that you will discover.

Emotional intelligence can be used for a number of things. Mastering it can better so many facets of an individual's life. When you have mastery of it, one tends to become more self-aware. This self-awareness also translates into better self-management. The key to becoming more connected with your emotions is to ensure that whatever you are feeling, you name it appropriately. This means if you are angry, do not mistake it for sadness. Accurately identify the emotion. You should then go ahead to attribute that particular emotion with the source that caused it. This is to ensure that you do not take out your emotions on the wrong sources. The next thing would be to curb yourself from acting out because of your emotions. This helps you in fostering emotional maturity. It also enables you to identify both your strengths and your weaknesses when it comes to your emotional intelligence.

Another thing that you would have to keep in mind when you are trying to understand what emotional intelligence is, would be figuring out what causes emotions in the first place. Understanding all the psychological factors that come in to play when your emotions are being formed are one way of enabling yourself to learn how to exploit those very emotions to work towards your personal development.

Managing your motions as well as your behavior in a better manner is also key in learning about emotional intelligence. This will involve improving how you self-regulate yourself. You would also have to learn how to manage your frustrations in smarter ways as this would be the one of the ways emotional intelligence would help you to reach the goals you have set for yourself.

Interacting better with people also helps an individual in enhancing their emotional intelligence. The stronger it is, the easier you find relating to other people. It not only makes an individual more empathetic but you also start identifying better with people. One way you can try and improve it when it comes to interactions with other people is by trying to become a better listener. This enables you to connect with the emotions that they are feeling and in turn you are better equipped at reacting to them in the appropriate manner. Having a better understanding of what is emotional intelligence will have an overall positive effect on your life.

People who've attained arts of emotional intelligence have quite a number of benefits working for them; for instance it is very possible for individuals who've attained such success to exude acts such as telepathy, mind reading and even healing abilities through the power of their minds. There is no limit to what an individual can attain through affecting power of their minds its only necessary for one to create an interest and a belief system that they can achieve what they desire to achieve through power in their minds. As earlier mentioned in seeing an explanation of what is emotional intelligence, people will have different sentiments and thoughts towards different meanings. However, attaining acts of emotional intelligence are very beneficial to any individual interested in attaining any life success.

TWO CONTRASTING STORIES OF EMOTIONAL INTELLIGENCE

Betty had a 162 IQ and spent a good deal of her time studying. She was bound and determined to get into Harvard and knew she had a good shot. She joined clubs not because she wanted to join or even had an interest, but because she knew it would look good on her Ivy League school application. During her high school career, while other kids were going to dances and enjoying themselves, Betty was spending all of her time studying. She was not only going to go to Harvard, she was also going to become a doctor and she wasn't allowing anything to stand in her way. Betty did have a few friends who she hung out with in school, but she was not considered popular. She longed to be able to fit in more with her peers, but felt that many of them were unintelligent. She found it increasingly difficult to form relationships with anyone. They just weren't as smart as her and she couldn't be forgiving. Besides, when she got to Harvard she would find more intelligent people like her.

Doug was in Betty's class. He never really noticed Betty but Betty sure noticed Doug. It seemed that everywhere Doug went, he attracted a crowd. He was gregarious and friendly to everyone he met and oozed charm. Doug was an average student, but was able to talk his way out of just about any type of trouble. Doug was elected class president and was voted "Most Popular" by the senior class. Skip forward 20 years. Betty went to Harvard, went to medical school and began practicing medicine. She still has a difficult time with her emotions and relating to other people. She married for a short while but it ended in divorce. She has a daughter who she is grooming to go to Harvard.

Doug started his own business after high school and never even went to college. He is a successful entrepreneur with a happy marriage and a house full of kids. He still keeps in touch with his high school classmates and is organizing the reunion. Ironically, he and Betty live in the same neighborhood. Their paths don't cross because Doug is still a social butterfly and Betty still chooses to remain aloof. Betty doesn't even know the names of her next door neighbors. Doug has been voted the homeowner's association president. Whose life seems more fulfilling? Most people would say that Doug's life seems to be the ideal life. The reason that they say this is because Doug is popular with other people. Despite her education and IQ, Betty seems to appear on a lower social rung than Doug. We often elevate people who are highly educated to higher rungs on the social ladder. They begin to slip down a few steps if they lack basic social skills. Many people, like Betty, did not bother learning social skills. Betty achieved her dream of going to Harvard and medical school but she has few patients who really like her. This is mostly due to her lack of empathy for people and being able to connect.

Most entrepreneurs and politicians have excellent social skills. People do not have to be overly educated in order to be well liked and successful. The late President, Ronald Reagan, did not have the education of many of his colleagues in politics, but he was able to run rings around them when it came to charm. And it was his charm that made him one of the most successful presidents of the 20th century. We want to emulate Doug's life because we are caring human beings. And human beings are social species who need social interactions to make them feel whole. Human beings are not content to be alone. This is why social skills are so important and why someone with stellar social skills will find that the sky is the limit as far as their goals and ambitions are concerned.

Can Emotional Intelligence Be Learned?

While EQ is relevant in almost any work situation where people work collaboratively, the use of EQ to improve leadership and managerial performance is of great interest to the HR community. And the current challenging economy has everyone trying to achieve more productivity with fewer resources. It's this desire for high performance that led Sales Training International Ltd to look more closely at EQ.

We constantly help organizations achieve higher performance through training and interpersonal skills development. Our experience with companies of all size shows that effective leaders can improve the performance of their organizations. Certainly different situations necessitate different leadership techni ues. And in practice a leader with good EQ skills is able to assess a situation and determine an appropriate response. Without EQ, a person with high IQ, great experience and good ideas will not become a great leader. And the higher a leader advances, the more important Emotional Intelligence becomes. But the potential for EQ problems also rises with more senior executives.

Research conducted by Fabio Sala showed that higher level executives consistently rated themselves higher on EQ competencies than did their lower-level colleagues. They have an inflated view of their EQ. Sala suggested that the rating difference may be related to a lack of objective information about their own skills, saying that senior executives typically have fewer opportunities for feedback because of their position and that people are often less inclined to give constructive feedback to people in positions senior to themselves.

BEING EMOTIONALLY INTELLIGENT

Our natural state of being, as one with Soul, is a harmonious state of Love, in which the only feelings are of continuous peace and bliss. Therefore if we are feeling any feeling other than peace and bliss, we have got out of balance somewhere. This is due to our conditioned and faulty thinking, which emerges as tolerations, needs and limiting beliefs. Using our Emotional Intelligence equips us to identify the message that Soul is sending us through these feelings, so we can rectify our thinking and thus move always towards Love.

Being Emotionally Intelligent is my ability to consciously comprehend my own emotional States of Being. Being 'Emotional' means that I am aware of the feeling that is my emotional state of being. Being 'Intelligent' means I have a rational knowledge or logical understanding of the situation, occurrence and circumstances that I am currently experiencing. I am Intelligent when I can consciously rationalize what is happening in my reality. I am Emotional when I can feel the awareness of my energetic state of being - my emotional energy.

Emotional Intelligence loses clarity when I confuse 'being emotional' with 'being irrational'. When I am studying negative states of being that cause me to sub-consciously react, I am learning about my own irrational behavior that is without emotional intelligence. I am studying 'irrational intelligence'.

Being emotional is not reacting irrationally; it is being consciously-aware of my emotional state of being. I never react emotionally because with emotional intelligence I am always able to respond intelligently. Negative emotional states of being are irrational because a rationally intelligent person who is emotionally

16

aware (intelligent) would never choose to experience them. Understanding irrational behavior does re□uire emotional intelligence but it is not the definition of Emotional Intelligence.

Emotional States Of Being

Emotional 'States of Being' re□uire definition before I can understand them intelligently. When I define an emotional state of being, I give it definition, it becomes a definite emotion, and I become consciously-aware of its existence.

It is my conscious-awareness of the definite nature of my emotions that allows me to be emotionally intelligent.

An 'Emotional' person is aware of their feelings as different emotions.

An 'Emotionally Intelligent' person is able to consciously name (define) their emotional state of being and create it at will, if and when they so choose. By intelligently defining an emotion, I become both emotionally aware of the feeling and rationally conscious of its definition. I cannot experience a definite emotion unless I can name it adjectively. In the absence of naming an emotion, it will remain either a positive or a negative experience, dependent on the beliefs that I hold in my sub-conscious.

I define an emotion (emotional state of being) with an adjective, which is a describing word. Any adjective that describes my feelings or my emotional state of being is an emotion. Without an adjective to describe it, an emotion is just a feeling that I don't really understand.

The Potential of my Emotional Energy

Emotion is an energetic state of being that I am experiencing. All forms of energy have a force, a magnitude and a potential. Emotions are no different. The potential of any energy is realized when the force and magnitude of that energy unite.

Electrical energy has a force called 'volts', a magnitude called 'amps' and a potential called 'watts'. They are all named after the person who first defined them. Emotional energy is more complicated because not only is its potential divided by force and magnitude but its force is divided by polarity and its magnitude is divided by gender.

The polarity of my emotions is either positive or negative and the gender of my energy is either male or female. (Anger & pride are male whereas meekness & humility are female. However, Impatience and intolerance are usually seen as negative and patience and tolerance as positive).

The degree, to which my emotional energy is unbalanced, by being divided by either polarity or gender or both, determines the intensity of the emotion that I am feeling. The greater is the imbalance the greater is the intensity of the emotional feeling. The intensity of my emotional state of being is the product of both the gender and the polarity of the emotional energy.

Emotional Intelligence re□uires not only the definition of my emotional state of being but the understanding of its potential for my Life.

Understanding the potential of my emotional energy requires me to be consciously-aware of:

- ✓ Its force and magnitude
- ✓ Its gender, polarity and intensity
- ✓ Its definition or Adjectively
- ✓ The sponsoring thought or thoughts that are creating the emotion.

The Ultimate Potential of my Emotional Energy is the Pure Feeling of Love that emanates from my Soul.

Life is an emotional experience

My Emotional Intelligence re□uires more than my ability to manage my irrational behavior. It re□uires the ability to understand my emotional experiences intelligently. The cause of my irrational behavior is my lack of emotional intelligence. I react irrationally with what is sometimes confusingly called an emotional reaction.

I respond with positive emotion once I attain the intelligence and understanding to do so. My symptoms of irrational behavior are created by my lack of rational intelligence. Extreme irrational behavior caused by a lack of rational ability may be diagnosed as a mental illness by a rational person who has no emotional intelligence.

Diagnosing emotional disorder or disease re□uires emotional intelligence not rational intelligence, which is probably why illness is usually diagnosed as either physical or mental and not emotional. In the absence of emotional intelligence, my life became an unemotional experience as a rationally intelligent man.

In a dualistic world, the more rationally intelligent I become the more contained, disconnected and emotionally unintelligent I am. It is my experience that the more I rationalize my world with tolerance and patience the less I react with the frustration of my anger and intolerance. However, with emotional intelligence I consciously choose to be 'Accepting' instead of tolerant and 'Allowing' instead of patient. I no longer choose to be a tolerant patient who is patiently tolerating Life.

I am now accepting Life as an emotional experience because I am learning to be emotionally intelligent enough to allow it to be so.

THE TRUE TEST OF EMOTIONAL INTELLIGENCE

The true test of my Emotional Intelligence is whether I can be Happy & Well as a result of my conscious choice to be so. It is only my emotional ignorance that is depriving me of the happiness and well-being that is my true nature.

Happiness is an emotional feeling. How can a rational man be happy in a state of being disconnected and unemotional? Well-being is an emotional feeling. How can I feel well in a society that medicates physical and mental illness without one iota of emotional intelligence?

Having compassion for other people doesn't mean anything unless I have defined the compassion that I am feeling. Defining compassion as: "Wanting to alleviate the suffering of others", is a rationally intelligent definition of a physical desire not the definition of an emotional feeling.

It is my lack of emotional intelligence that disconnects me from my true emotional nature. A logical world has become an unemotional world that is devoid of true Happiness & Well-being and is full of sadness and sickness. We have lost our connection to our true Wealth and our true Health when, as a society, we are disconnected from our Emotional Intelligence.

In an emotionally intelligent society, the only irrational behavior is to be unemotional and intellectually challenged by one's own emotional experiences. The challenge of a new society is for men to become emotionally-rational and for women to become rationally-emotional and for both to understand that there is no distinction between the two. The battle of the Sexes will then be declared as over.

WHY IS EMOTIONAL INTELLIGENCE SO IMPORTANT?

Many people are not completely aware how important emotional intelligence is in their lives. We attempt to read many books and articles about this matter just for the knowledge, but we ignore the fact that if we apply emotional intelligence in our daily life and work, it could lead us to somewhere else that we never expected.

The key skills of emotional intelligence could be learned by anyone, at any time. Imagine if you are able to overcome, control and get over your daily life stress with just being emotionally aware of everything that goes right there around you.

Emotional intelligence could be summarized in the ability to express your emotions and to control them at the same time, understand and interpret to others feelings.

There are four easy steps that can lead you to the emotional intelligence you always wished to have;

The first one is sensing the emotions: you should concentrate and accurately perceive the message someone tries to tell you, this actually involves not only understanding the person's intended words but also watching the non-verbal signs, body language and facial expressions.

The second one is reasoning with emotions: we should use our emotions to promote thinking. Emotions help in prioritizing what we pay attention and react to. This means that emotions play a very big part in guiding our minds to believing things that might or might not happen. We naturally react to things that attract our minds.

The third one is understanding emotions: emotions may carry whole different meanings at many times, some people can express their anger in an indirect way, this can actually be very obvious in the example of the angry boss; he can scream, shout and give you a very hard time just because he has an issue related to your work, or he experienced a bad morning with his wife. We should never get confused in understanding the reasons behind people's reactions and that's why training yourself to have emotional intelligence can help you in this matter.

The fourth and last one is managing emotions (the ability to manage your emotions): Emotions are valuable, and offer a bounty of benefits. Once we're able to process and cope with them effectively, we can then learn a lot about ourselves and our needs. If you feel something, let it out, do not engage yourself in another action hoping you can distract your feelings; this can lead you to many problems.

Managing and controlling your emotions and feelings are very important; it is a step towards reaching the emotional intelligence of knowing how to perfectly understand people around you with the least words and actions they make.

Some people see emotional intelligence as an inborn characteristic and others say it could be learned and strengthened, as for me, I can definitely say that it can easily be learned and practiced. You may face some difficulties at first, but with trying many times, it will at the end easily work.

As we know, it's not the smartest people who are the most successful or the most fulfilled in life. You probably know people who are academically brilliant and yet are socially inept and unsuccessful at work or in their personal relationships. Intellectual ability or your intelligence quotient (IQ) isn't enough on its own to achieve success in life. Yes, your IQ can help you get into college, but it's your EQ that will help you manage the stress and emotions when facing your final exams. IQ and EQ exist in tandem and are most effective when they build off one another.

Emotional intelligence affects:

Your performance at school or work. High emotional intelligence can help you navigate the social complexities of the workplace, lead and motivate others, and excel in your career. In fact, when it comes to gauging important job candidates, many companies now rate emotional intelligence as important as technical ability and employ EQ testing before hiring.

Your physical health. If you're unable to manage your emotions, you are probably not managing your stress either. This can lead to serious health problems. Uncontrolled stress raises blood pressure, suppresses the immune system, increases the risk of heart attacks and strokes, contributes to infertility, and speeds up the aging process. The first step to improving emotional intelligence is to learn how to manage stress.

Your mental health. Uncontrolled emotions and stress can also impact your mental health, making you vulnerable to anxiety and depression. If you are unable to understand, get comfortable with, or manage your emotions, you'll also struggle to form strong relationships. This in turn can leave you feeling lonely and isolated and further exacerbate any mental health problems.

Your relationships. By understanding your emotions and how to control them, you're better able to express how you feel and understand how others are feeling. This allows you to communicate more effectively and forge stronger relationships, both at work and in your personal life.

Your social intelligence. Being in tune with your emotions serves a social purpose, connecting you to other people and the world around you. Social intelligence enables you to recognize friend from foe, measure another person's interest in you, reduce stress, balance your nervous system through social communication, and feel loved and happy.

EMOTIONAL INTELLIGENCE SKILLS HAPPEN INSIDE YOUR BRAIN FIRST

Emotional Intelligence Skills involve brain fitness? According to Simon Evans, Ph.D. and Paul Burghardt, Ph.D., the answer is yes, and here is what they say.

"1. Emotional Intelligence (EQ). Your brain controls your mood and your ability to handle stress and respond to challenges. It controls your ability to read the emotions of others and respond appropriately. Your emotional intelligence, or EQ, is the aspect of brain fitness that has a large impact on your self-confidence, day to day mood and success in social environments, including career and family life. For the most part, a system in your brain called your cortico-limbic system is responsible for controlling your emotional intelligence, and like most systems in your brain, you can improve it with specific focus."

First Emotional Intelligence Skill

So if we follow the Evans and Burghardt line of thought, the first emotional intelligence skill to work on is taking care of your brain.

That involves keeping your brain rested, fed, exercised, relaxed, and yet challenged with novel learning experiences.

When I routinely handle those basic health kinds of tasks, my brain, the master integrator of everything I do including emotional intelligence, will be very plastic, in other words, it will be constantly rewiring itself and creating new connections due to the changing emotional landscapes around me, and that brain will also be manufacturing new brain cells for my brain at the maximum daily amount allowed, which is called neurogenesis.

New neurons, according to my reading of the research, routinely end up at the hippocampus, which is part of the cortico-limbic system mentioned by Evans and Burghardt above.

There is lots of information in their book, Brainfit for Life, about the how to's of nutrition, sleep, and physical exercise, and there is an excellent discussion of what novel learning experiences can be.

Emotional Intelligence Happens Internally and Externally

Once the brain is fit, now we can begin to discuss the discreet skills of emotional intelligence.

Once again, I must work inside me first, with self-talk.

As a domestic violence educator, I work with folks who are not committed to emotional intelligence, or they do not know how to emotional intelligence, and I teach first, basic self-talk skills.

When I am heading into group, and I have done thousands of them, I need to reaffirm, with self-talk, inside my head that I am going to listen respectfully, even though I have no idea how I will be spoken to. I suggest to my clients that they do the same, make some self-talk commitments to themselves.

When I am going home, I need to make another mental commitment to myself to listen to my wife, who will want to talk about her day and our children and her plans for flower beds and the deck, etc.

I know that I do not need to agree or disagree with anything she says, I just need to listen, which is a skill with discrete steps, and is very learnable.

When I listen, I give the Gift of Attention, which leaves my wife, and the people I listened to feeling a bit of contentment.

Remember, you do not need to agree or disagree, just listen, maybe even turn your head to the side and give them your ear.

When I make that internal statement to myself that I will listen, I feel calm, and that calmness impacts the speaker, who may be very loud, which simply means they want to be heard.

So the first emotional intelligence skill is to say to yourself, fairly fre□uently, and this will be □uick, I am going to practice emotional intelligence skills, like listening.

Why do you need to do that fre□uently? Because the human orienting response will pull you away □uickly. We are hard wired to respond to movement in the environment, and when I look towards the window where there was just a flash of light, I may forget the commitment I had made and join in the argument because my very healthy brain processes data at the rate of 7 bits every 1/18th second.

It changes thoughts fast.

The next emotional intelligence skill I need to attend to is managing my own feelings.

That involves awareness that thoughts change feelings, so if I am experiencing an unpleasant feeling I need to change the thought to change the feeling, or take a deep breath, or do my heart rate variability biofeedback.

Again we are working in the personal aspects of emotional intelligence, so that I can operate effectively, cooperatively and affiliativly, in the external relationship.

It is my belief, that emotional intelligence skills happen inside me first, and need to be managed at the rate of my Central Nervous System and that is a very fast management.

Chapter One

THE ART OF CONTROLLING YOUR EMOTIONS

To live a better and happier life, you must take charge of the natural instinctive state of your mind arising from circumstances, moods or relationships with others. Controlling your emotions doesn't mean ignoring them, it means you recognize and take rightful actions on them. You must be in-charge of your emotions day-to-day! If you truly desire unlimited happiness, you must control your emotions. Do you struggle to control your emotions?

Do you feel like you can't seem to control your emotions? Maybe you lash out at others around you and later feel bad about it. If you're like me, you're thinking that's something is wrong with you because you just can't seem to control your emotions. You have the power to create your state of blissful and favorable emotional circumstances. A clear mind is better and able to control emotions. Un-clutter your mind!

One day I would wake up crying feeling all emotional and then the next day I'm happy as to be. I use to think that I was bi-polar or something because of how my emotions would shift from time to time. I would lash out at whoever was around me and wouldn't think twice about it. There was a time in my life when others thought I was unable to feel emotions because I acted as if I didn't care about nothing, and nothing seem to affect me. Why is that?

Why do some people feel like they can't control their emotions? Why do others act as if they're unable to feel anything?

A lot of people allow their emotions to control them. They allow their emotions to dictate how they are going to feel this day. They allow their emotions to tell them how to act when someone make them mad. Let's take anger for an example. You may be struggling with anger issues, and you constantly feel like there is something wrong with you for feeling anger all of the time. Anger is just an emotion. Anger is place inside of us to help us know when someone is taking advantage of us and when something is not right. We are not to act on anger, but it is normal to feel anger. God wants us to learn how to control our anger. The bible says "In your anger do not sin". God do not want you to walk around always mad about something. He want you to get to the root of what's causing you so much anger in the first place

Emotion is the generic term for subjective or conscious experience that is characterized by psycho-physiological expressions, biological reactions and mental states. It is often associated and considered reciprocally influential with temperament, personality, mood, motivation and depression. Emotions can be influenced by hormones and alcohol. It is the force behind human actions and reactions. Emotions can be expressed in the form of fear, joy, envy, excitement, distrust, depression, curiosity, contentment, desire, despair, embarrassment, confidence, gratitude, happiness, shame and shock.

With the harsh weather conditions, the economy in a miserable state, lack of job security, infidel partner, stubborn children, nagging co-workers, and unrest in the society, it can be easy to allow your emotions to run amok. An uncontrolled state of mind can make a bad situation worse. Every emotion begins with a thought. If you learn to control your mind and thoughts, you can rule your emotions. Guard your heart because out of it flows the issues of life. As you think in your heart, so you are. While it does take practice, you can be in firm control of any of the particular feelings that characterize the state of your mind, such as hate, horror, anger, fear, happiness or love.

Have you ever met an emotionless person? They seem like they don't feel anything inside. They hide their emotions from others to see. People who have been so hurt so badly in their past put up walls around them and adopt this emotionless demeanor about themselves. They can feel pain just like we do, they just unable to show them. I was this type of person and I notice how some of my friends would say stuff like, "what's wrong with you. You act like you don't even care about nothing". That was my way of not allowing me to get hurt again. I train myself to respond that way toward people. I still felt pain inside. I just didn't show them my pain.

If you want to know how to control your emotions, this is what you should remember - trying to control your emotions is a hard thing and to a large extent, unnecessary. The key is to let them be and instead choose your reaction to them.

Emotions are not our enemies, they are our friends, and even the negative ones are here to help us. They act as guideposts to show us the direction where we need to go. They make us human and help us in decision making process.

If you would need to logically calculate every little decision, it would make life way too hard. Also it would be nearly impossible. How would you logically explain, whether to watch "Die Hard 3" or "Princess Diaries". Impossible. You just trust your gut instinct and choose upon your emotions at the time.

If you are overwhelmed by them and there are important decisions at stake, let them be and postpone decision making. Important decisions are better to be made in a peaceful state.

It is necessary to stay connected to them at all times. You are always bigger than your emotions, your thoughts and emotions cannot hurt you. They are in you, but not you. You are something higher, something separate from them.

Thoughts and emotions are not obligations to act. After feeling the emotions, there is a gap, this is the place where you can choose your reaction to them. This gap is the place where you are able to determine the course of your life.

Think what is the outcome you want and then act in a way that gives you that outcome. Preferably the outcome should be something that reduces the amount of negative emotions arising.

Do not identify yourself with your emotions, be the Observer of them. The Observer sees, acknowledges, but does not react. The Observer acts. Always act, but never react. By reacting you are usually replaying the situation and reinforcing it. By acting you are in charge of the course of your life.

This is easier said than done. Especially when being overwhelmed by them we ask the question- how to control your emotions? This is not the right question to ask. Right question to ask would be- how could I improve the situation?

Emotions are here to be heard and felt through. When being overwhelmed, it sometimes means that they were repressed and in order for you to hear them, they needed to make a stronger statement.

If you let them be they start to lose their strength, like being convinced that they have been heard. After that you can be more peaceful and start taking real action to improve the situation. This way of life needs some practice. People tend to be reactive, but being reactive can throw us off course.

Learning to control your emotions during challenging times of emotional stress is beneficial to your mental and general health. Emotions play a great role in life, and decisions are often based on feelings. However, problems occur when emotions are out of control. Becoming a master of emotional intelligence which involves emotional literacy, emotional coping and emotional awareness will help improve your emotional sagacity which helps you develop a good emotional freedom technique. To go higher in your career, build good relationships with people and be successful in life, you must keep a tab on your emotional quotient. It is common in day-to-day life to regret those actions we took because of uncontrolled emotion.

KNOWING YOUR EMOTIONS

What would life be like without our emotions? Kind of boring? Like a flat soda? Without that fizz and sparkle, we wouldn't be very interested in drinking life in. Emotions bring energy, color and variety to our lives, but we also spend a lot of time confused by them. They can transport us to blissful, peak states and drag us down to the depths of delusion and despair — and everything in between.

People are driven by their emotions to marry each other and to murder each other (sadly, sometimes the very same person they married!). Every day we get in line for this roller coaster ride of emotion that thrills us one minute and turns us upside down the next. What are these unpredictable feelings and why do they seem to control us, rather than the other way around?

It depends on who you ask. You'll get a different answer from a scientist, a therapist, a priest, an artist, or the usual beneficiaries of your love and loathing – your family and frenemies. There's an Asian proverb that says: "Medicine, if taken with knowledge; poison, if abused." This is how our emotions are. If we learn how to relate to our emotions skillfully, then they're like medicine, containing great wisdom; but if we lack this understanding, then they're like poison, causing great harm and suffering. While we're under the spell of our emotions, it's like we're sick. We can't wish away the aches and pains and fever. You have to let your sickness run its course or intervene with some kind of treatment.

If you understand your illness, you can take steps to heal yourself and end your suffering. But if you don't know what you're doing – if you take the wrong medicine – you could make yourself sicker. In the same way, when you understand your emotions and what makes them tick, you can work with their intense energy and start to heal your suffering.

Your emotions are crucial to your ability to adapt to the challenges of your daily life. When you feel good, you're able to shrug off even the most burdensome of tasks, but when you're miserable, you view even an enjoyable activity with a sense of gloom and doom. Emotions also affect our relationships with others. If a friend tells you a tragic story and you react by snickering instead of looking sad or concerned, you'll seem rude and insensitive. On the other hand, if you frown when you should smile at your friend's jokes, you'll cause offense for different reasons.

Flying off the handle to a minor annoyance can make you seem hyper or even unbalanced. Conversely, if you react with undue glee to a relatively minor piece of good news, people will also question your maturity and stability. Babies are allowed to shriek with pleasure or howl with rage but as adults, we're expected to rein in the outward show of our feelings.

If you need more convincing about the role of emotions in our ability to succeed or fail in facing life's challenges, think about some of the famous people whose careers have been undone by the improper show of their feelings. In the primary run up to the 2004 presidential election, Howard Dean's candidacy ended virtually overnight after his "YAAAAHHH" moment became an overnight Internet sensation. Edmund Muskie, in the 1972 primary season, committed a similar political gaffe in which he shed tears after winning the New Hampshire primary (though he claimed they were snowflakes shimmering in the morning light). Ironically, tears are all the rage in the post-2000 political world. Hillary Clinton wasn't considered sympathetic enough until her eyes misted over while answering a voter's □uestion (again in New Hampshire!), but many pundits used this against her to question her sincerity. Then there's the sentimental carryings-on of House Republican leader John Boehner, whose tear ducts seem on constant overdrive.

These examples show not only that the outward display of inner feelings influences how we're regarded by others, but also that these emotional displays are heavily dependent on cultural norms. To be regarded as a well-adapted member of society we need to adhere to those norms or risk condemnation or ridicule. Psychologist Paul Ekman showed that there are six basic emotions that people of all cultures experience and recognize (happiness, sadness, surprise, anger, fear, and disgust). How and when we express these emotions differs radically by the norms of each of our cultures, the so-called display rules.

Our emotions affect not only the way others treat us, but our inner sense of well-being. We tend to believe that whether we are experiencing positive or negative emotions reflects forces outside our control, blaming everything from our genes to the weather. However, what many people do not realize is that emotions aren't strictly controlled by your body's physiology the way that reflexes are. You're not stuck for life with the emotional e uipment programmed into your DNA.

To understand the way that you can control your emotions, we first have to take a slight detour through the early history of psychology. Views about what emotions are, and what causes them, have changed radically in the last 100 or so years. To take this journey, who better to start with than William James, the founder of American psychology? According to James, and the closely related views of physiologist Carl Lange, your emotions are completely governed by your body's responses.

In fact, they are the emotions. Imagine you're being pursued by a bear. If you're like most of us, fear and panic will take over your entire being, causing your heart to race, your palms to get sweaty, and your stomach to turn somersaults. James and Lange equated these responses of your autonomic nervous system with the actual emotion of fear.

According to their theory (known to intro psych students as the infamous "James-Lange Theory"), your bodily reaction doesn't follow the emotion, it is the emotion. As James said, "Common sense says we lose our fortune, are sorry and weep; we meet a bear, are frightened and run; we are insulted by a rival, are angry and strike, afraid because we tremble... the more rational statement is that we feel sorry because we cry, angry because we strike, afraid because we tremble" (Ellsworth, 1994, p. 222). Quite literally, when James and Lange talked about a "visceral" (or gut) emotional reaction, they meant it.

Many people found the James-Lange theory hard to accept. Common sense seems to work out just fine, despite James' assertion. Apart from the theory just "feeling" wrong (so to speak), it also failed to meet the test of scientific acceptability and was therefore eventually dropped as an explanation.

One very similar theory that appeared soon after the James-Lange foray into the field was that proposed by physiologist Walter Cannon; a view that is now known as the "Cannon-Bard" theory (reflecting his collaboration with a doctoral student named Philip Bard). This theory proposes that our emotions are regulated by the reaction of a small structure in the brain known as the thalamus. It's the thalamus that would sense, for example, the onrushing bear. This sensation simultaneously causes the visceral reactions in the body and the subjective experience in the brain. The Cannon-Bard theory eventually became discredited too because it did not withstand experimental scrutiny. The thalamus may be involved in some emotional regulation, but it's not the brain's hot spot for our feelings. Instead, the amygdala seems to be the culprit when it comes to such emotions as fear, rage, and jealousy.

The idea that our emotions may be controllable started to emerge in the theory developed by Stanley Schachter and Jerome Singer in the early 1960s. In their now classic psychology experiment, they led college students to believe that they were receiving a trial dose of a vitamin. In fact, the experimenters injected the students with epinephrine. The students then watched a "confederate" (another student acting out experimental instructions) who became either angry or euphoric while completing a set of ⬚uestionnaires. The students exposed to the angry confederate reported that they felt angry; those exposed to the euphoric confederate said they felt happy. The results showed that the combination of arousal (caused by epinephrine) and context (the confederate's behavior) influenced the emotional state of the experimental subject.

To translate, the Schachter-Singer study implies that your emotions are influenced by what's going on in the people around you and which emotions they're expressing. Another term for this is "emotional contagion." If you've ever felt moved to cry at the wedding of people you don't know very well because everyone around you is weeping into their hankies, you know how these feelings can catch on. (Why we cry at weddings is another story.)

Your emotions don't have to fall prey to those being expressed by the people around you, though. The cognitive revolution in emotion theory, led by University of Pennsylvania psychiatrist Aaron Beck, showed that our thoughts alone can produce our emotions. Beck's studies of depressed individuals led him to the discovery that dysfunctional attitudes and negatively-framed automatic thoughts are at the root of people's feelings of sadness. A dysfunctional attitude is a way of viewing the world that focuses on the negative and unrealistic aspects of your experiences. A negatively-framed automatic thought is an unconscious belief that focuses on your weaknesses rather than your strengths. Together, dysfunctional attitudes and automatic thoughts create the "negative triad" consisting of a negative view of yourself, your world, and your future. The extensive research based on Beck's theory has led to acceptance of his cognitive-behavioral method of therapy as the premier treatment of depression.

Even if you're not clinically depressed, you can borrow a page from Beck's playbook to understand your emotions. For instance, sadness is caused by the belief that you've lost or will lose something important to you, anger is caused by the belief that someone has taken something away from you, and anxiety is based on the belief that something bad will happen to you. Unrealistically distorting your experiences produces these thoughts which then lead to your negative emotions.

Rational-emotive psychologist Albert Ellis takes another approach to cognitive theory, accounting more broadly for our tendencies to let our thoughts produce our own self-produced misery. Ellis believed that through "musturbation" we allow our emotions to be dominated by the "must's": "I must be successful," "I must be loved," "I must have what I want." Ellis talked about the "A-B-C" model of emotion:

A: Activating event (a friend turns you down for dinner)

+B: Belief (no one likes me)

=C: Consequence (sad mood, feelings of rejection)

To change the conse□uence (i.e. your emotion), you need to change your beliefs. To change your beliefs you need to examine them. In this example, you can the belief that "no one likes me" by looking at the evidence for this belief. Why do you think that no one likes you? Does one person's turning you down mean that no one likes you? Does this mean that no one will ever like you? Does it mean that you must have everyone like you? (This is "musturbation.")

It's through challenging your thoughts and beliefs about yourself that you can change your emotional reactions. Once you start to pick apart the illogical basis for your emotions you can free yourself from being dominated by the maladaptive emotions of rage, jealousy, rejection, and dejection and instead boost your adaptive emotions of happiness, contentment, and joy.

Now that you've given your thoughts this readjustment, you've got one more job to do. According to the "facial feedback hypothesis" of emotion, the expression on your face can influence your emotional state. When you activate the muscles that control your facial expressions, you actually trigger internal changes that lead to the corresponding mood. If you frown, you'll feel mad. If you turn the corners of your mouth down, you'll feel sad. And if you turn the corners of your mouth up in a smile you'll feel good.

41

As the song says, to "make gray skies clear up," just "put on a happy face!"

With this emotional repair kit, you'll be able to make more than the gray skies clear up. You don't have to be held hostage to your gut, your thalamus, or even your amygdala. Focus on the thoughts that precede your emotions and you'll find that you can control your mood. And remember to smile!

To get real help with emotions, we have to go beyond a simple textbook understanding of them. It isn't enough just to know how many and what kinds of emotions there are. When we strip away what we think we know and look freshly at our personal experience of anger or passion or jealousy, what do we find? This is not just about recognizing what kind of thoughts we're having. It's about discovering what our emotions are at their very core. Seeing that anger makes us want to strike back or that desire makes us want to please is just the beginning. Really getting to know our emotions is challenging, but it can be motivating too. When we see that we're continually getting beat up by our emotions — we can become determined to learn how to rescue ourselves.

MANAGING YOUR EMOTIONS

I was having a chat with a friend recently who declared that her emotional outbursts are not often "useful" in some circumstance. I asked her what she meant by "useful?" She suggested when one feels emotionally driven to speak their mind, it may not be conducive in producing a positive result. You see, an emotion is an "absolute" entity taking shape within us. We do not question the validity of the emotion - I like that person, I dislike that jumper, I love chocolate ice-cream! These are emotions based on preferences we like.

Emotions are based on the beliefs you've formed over the years. Take a moment and think about a belief you hold true for you. One of mine is "I believe the world is a beautiful place and every experience I have is neither good nor bad, yet there is a great lesson contained within it." Yes it is a rather long belief isn't?!

Now if I examine my belief and ask myself when I formed my belief and what circumstances were behind it, I find that it goes back some years. My belief is based on my experience of having personally gone through a life threatening illness and losing a family member to a debilitating disease. Given those two occurrences, I am still able to see the beauty, mystery and lessons in life unfold. I have attached an emotion around that belief which brings me joy and bliss for being able to get up every morning to speak and communicate my experience, lessons and knowledge to people all over the world.

Our emotions can serve to lift us to great heights or hinder our personal growth. One of the mechanisms which may become useful with managing your emotions is to become mindful or aware of them as they occur. For many people, they remain asleep when it comes to the nature of their emotions; the role they serve in their life. Through repeated exposure of learning to identify and manage your emotions, you have a better understanding of how they may best serve you. It takes time, patience and perseverance.

Examine your emotions. What emotions are serving you right now? Are they useful? In order to understand the emotion and possibly reframe it, you need to examine the belief behind it - for that is the fuel. If the emotion is one of sadness, anger or anxiety, look closely at whether it is serving your greatest growth. The Buddhist principle states if the emotion is not necessary "drop it - put it down" as though it were a backpack. It's meant to be as simple as that, yet not quite so in practise.

If you find yourself flying off the handle when a loved one does the wrong thing by you, examine the emotion. Speak to it - "what do you want me to know or learn anger?" Look back to the belief surrounding the emotion. I can assure you that your loved one isn't the cause or the trigger of your emotion. It's the meaning you attached to it when he/she forgot to ring you while they were travelling interstate on business. You attached a meaning and assigned an emotion to it, which served an outcome - whether positive or negative.

When you're living in alignment with your true self, you develop a deep understanding and relationship with self. You're in alignment with your emotions, thoughts and beliefs. They begin to serve you, rather than work against you. You develop inner peace, harmony, joy and bliss. You radiate passion, enthusiasm - those around you are drawn to you like a moth to a flame. Begin now.

Take ownership of your life. Invest time and patience in getting to know you. You'll attract the most amazing relationships (business, personal, professional, intimate, friendship) and create a life worthy of prosperity and abundance.

5 Proven Ways To Manage Your Emotions

Your ability to regulate those emotions, in turn, affects how you're perceived by the people around you. If you're laughing at that text during a serious meeting, you're likely to get resentful looks from others in the room. On the other hand, if you react with rage at a driver who cuts you off in traffic, you can engender unwanted attention, and perhaps even risk your life.

The study of emotions is not an exact science. Psychologists still debate the body-mind connection in emotional reactivity; don't have a complete taxonomy of emotions; and are even uncertain about whether emotions are the cause or result of the way we construe the world. However, there are advances being made in understanding the concept of emotion regulation, the process of influencing the way emotions are felt and expressed.

Stanford University psychologist James Gross (2001) proposed a 4-stage model to capture the sequence of events that occurs when our emotions are stimulated. In what he calls the "modal model," a situation grabs our attention, which in turns leads us to appraise or think about the meaning of the situation. Our emotional responses result from the way we appraise our experiences.

Some emotional responses re□uire no particular regulation. If the emotion is appropriate to the situation and helps you feel better, there's no need to worry about changing the way you handle things. Laughing when others are laughing is one example of an appropriate reaction that helps you feel better. Expressing road rage may also make you feel better, but it's not appropriate or particularly adaptive. You could express your frustration in other ways that allow you to release those angry feelings, or instead try to find a way to calm yourself down.

Calming yourself down when you're frustrated, of course, may be more easily said than done. If you tend to fly off the handle when aggravated and express your outrage to everyone within earshot (or on the other end of an email), your emotions could be costing you important relationships, your job, and even your health.

An inability to regulate emotions is, according to Gross and his collaborator Hooria Jazaieri (2014), at the root of psychological disorders such as depression and borderline personality disorder. Although more research is needed to understand the specific role of emotional regulation in psychopathology, this seems like a promising area of investigation. For example, people with social anxiety disorder can benefit from interventions that help them change the way they appraise social situations, as shown by research on cognitive behavioral therapy. Many others functioning at a less than optimal level of psychological health, Gross and Jazaieri maintain, could similarly benefit from education about how better to manage their emotions in daily life.

Fortunately, you can handle most of the work involved in regulating your emotions well before the provoking situation even occurs. By preparing yourself ahead of time, you'll find that the problematic emotion goes away before it interferes with your life:

Select the situation. Avoid circumstances that trigger unwanted emotions. If you know that you're most likely to get angry when you're in a hurry (and you become angry when others force you to wait), then don't leave things for the last minute. Get out of the house or office 10 minutes before you need to, and you won't be bothered so much by pedestrians, cars, or slow elevators. Similarly, if there's an acquaintance you find completely annoying, then figure out a way to keep from bumping into that person.

Modify the situation. Perhaps the emotion you're trying to reduce is disappointment. You're always hoping, for example, to serve the "perfect" meal for friends and family, but invariably something goes wrong because you've aimed too high. Modify the situation by finding recipes that are within your range of ability so that you can pull off the meal. You may not be able to construct the ideal soufflé, but you manage a pretty good frittata.

Shift your attention focus. Let's say that you constantly feel inferior to the people around you who always look great. You're at the gym, and can't help but notice the regulars on the weight machines who manage to lift three times as much as you can. Drawn to them like a magnet, you can't help but watch with wonder and envy at what they're able to accomplish. Shifting your focus away from them and onto your fellow gym rats who pack less punch will help you feel more confident about your own abilities. Even better, focus on what you're doing, and in the process, you'll eventually gain some of the strength you desire.

Change your thoughts. At the core of our deepest emotions are the beliefs that drive them. You feel sad when you believe to have lost something, anger when you decide that an important goal is thwarted, and happy anticipation when you believe something good is coming your way. By changing your thoughts you may not be able to change the situation but you can at least change the way you believe the situation is affecting you. In cognitive reappraisal, you replace the thoughts that lead to unhappiness with thoughts that lead instead to joy or at least contentment. People with social anxiety disorder may believe that they'll make fools of themselves in front of others for their social gaffes. They can be helped to relax by interventions that help them recognize that people don't judge them as harshly as they believe.

Change your response. If all else fails and you can't avoid, modify, shift your focus, or change your thoughts, and that emotion comes pouring out, the final step in emotion regulation is to get control of your response. Your heart may be beating out a steady drumroll of unpleasant sensations when you're made to be anxious or angry. Take deep breaths and perhaps close your eyes in order to calm yourself down. Similarly, if you can't stop laughing when everyone else seems serious or sad, gather your inner resources and force yourself at least to change your facial expression if not your mood.

This 5-step approach is one that you can readily adapt to the most characteristic situations that cause you trouble. Knowing your emotional triggers can help you avoid the problems in the first place. Being able to alter your thoughts and reactions will build your confidence in your own ability to cope. With practice, you'll be able to turn negatives into positives, and, each time, gain emotional fulfillment.

Homework:

Ask Yourself:

1. What emotions am I experiencing in this moment?

2. What does this emotion really mean for me?

3. Are my actions appropriate for this situation?

4. Am I stuck in an emotional rut?

5. Are my emotions prohibiting me from achieving my dreams?

Notice your emotions and dig a little deeper to see if you can get to the root of the cause. Then ask yourself the critical questions that can help you recognize the emotional patterns that may be kidnapping your goals. Taking these steps can put you on the path to maximizing your life.

Chapter Two

READING AND UNDERSTANDING THE EMOTIONS OF OTHERS: EMPATHY

The homeless man stood on the street corner in a ragged coat that was much too thin for the brisk winter day. He looked weary as he held up a simple cardboard sign that read, "Down on my luck. Anything helps." As we walked by, our small group of friends and acquaintances paused to give the man several dollars.

Most of us felt instant empathy and compassion for the man. Except one acquaintance's husband, who stood back in disgust ranting that the homeless were just freeloaders skilled at working the system. "He probably makes more money than I do," he continued to rage as we walked away. The acquaintance averted her eyes, embarrassed by her husband's cold, callous behavior.

Why is it that when we see another person suffering, some of us are able to instantly envision ourselves in the other person's place and feel sympathy for their pain while others remain indifferent and uncaring?

Empathy is the key.

WHAT IS EMPATHY?

Empathy is the ability to emotionally put oneself into someone else's shoes-the capacity to share and understand the feelings, emotions, and perspective experienced by another person, both negative and positive. Empathy is the identification and relationship that connects us as human beings.

We are generally pretty well-attuned to our own feelings and emotions. But empathy allows us to "walk a mile in another's shoes," so to speak. It permits us to understand the emotions that another person is feeling.

For many of us, seeing another person in pain and responding with indifference or even outright hostility seems utterly incomprehensible. But the fact that some people do respond in such a way clearly demonstrates that empathy is not a universal response to the suffering of others.

Sometimes to others, your life may seem to be really great, or even amazing, though that's until you have to navigate decisions that are not as apparent as they may seem, by someone else's eyes. Your eyes are yours, just as my eyes are mine, though sometimes, I'd like to be able to see what you can see, that I can't!

You would like to reach out, as if touching a cloud, to find a gentle hand, one that is reaching back, offering guidance, to lead you, support you, or to at least show you empathy.

Of one thing you can be certain: It is never wrong to ask for help, seek another's opinion, or at least to analyses the input of another individual's experience. Seeking the attention or assistance from someone who may be more experienced in life, than you, or I, could be of great help or amazing service! We have all experienced situations that are tumultuous, at best. At times, for no reason or rhyme: we are targeted, like a specimen, for a coveted skill or talent that is exploited or abused, for no apparent reason other than irrefutable covetousness.

We ARE all placed on the planet to provide a gift or service, first to ourselves, by having pride in our talent, work-ethic or ability to be original or creative, then to aid humanity, by any way that comes to us naturally. Ways of service may come about as a trait, discipline or skill that we have been taught or that comes to us innately, or even organically. Some of the most amazing skills that people demonstrate are totally and completely from within their own psyche. Take for example the skills of kindness, compassion and yes, even empathy is a great skill to have! You may not see these as skills, but indeed they are because, let's face facts, not everyone demonstrates them.

Did you know that empathy is not as natural for some people as you would expect it to be? Empathy is a feeling of compassion for your fellow-man, animal, or anything or anyone on this grand planet of ours. It is our job to engage others with empathy, and to show love and kindness to everyone and everything.

Understanding the power of empathy opens so many doors for you and for me and for others in our periphery! Empathy is a global and noble calling that enables understanding, helpful acts of kindness or sheer comfort to an otherwise uncomfortable life, circumstance, or haunting situation.

Make seeking or donating empathy more of an occasion, without expectation, show empathy to the hurt, downtrodden or even to the most undeserving of human beings. Its okay to feel and act upon empathy. Empathy is a far better skill to demonstrate than covetousness, fear, judgments or jealousy. It will bring you understanding and help resolve different viewpoints, or even give you more patience when presented with impractical situations.

Sometimes we get thrust into situations for ubiquitous reasons that have no rhyme or reason. The best thing is to show yourself empathy, even if nobody else will. Quiet your mind, even when someone or a group of people are denying that they are causing you anguish or disdain. They are being covetous over your work, written words or your ability to hone a skill that they themselves have not even tried to do for themselves. If they would at least try, they would understand that honing a skill takes take and effort and cannot be regained and should not be repackaged or reworded.

Turn that negative energy's direction around, toss it upside down!

Time to begin anew! Make this agonizing time ripe for resolution and solutions by planting and planning in fertile ways. Realize what is happening, re-purpose your thoughts and align with your mind, it is now the best time to focus on another avenue.

Learn to flourish throughout your pain and watch your life, focus and energy change. Life change can come in new and in even better ways! BE mindful that better days are ahead of you and bad days are now behind you. Let that soak in your thoughts and know it to be your truth. Focus on someone else, someone other than you...

This is best accomplished when helping others, especially those who need to land safely after a fall; you can show empathy by assisting them to land with both feet on the ground. Surround them with comfort, after they have experienced emotional turmoil or unresolved strife. Suffering through strife is not an easy feat, something both you and me understand completely, especially if you are someone who is sensitive and feels the pain and suffering of others, as well as his own pain. Strive cannot ever be completely removed, just as assured as are the life of our oceans and waves in our lives, though it can be analyzed.

When your life is at a crossroad and you don't know whether to turn to the left or to the right, don't make a move at all!!

WHY WE SOMETIMES LACK EMPATHY

As the story in the beginning of the article illustrated, not everyone experiences empathy in every situation. My acquaintance's husband felt no sympathy, empathy, or compassion for the homeless man shivering on a cold winter street, and even expressed outright hostility toward him. So why is that we feel empathy for some people but not for others? A number of different factors play a role. How we perceive the other person, how we attribute their behaviors, what we blame for the other person's predicament, and our own past experiences and expectations all come into play.

At the most basic level, there appear to be two main factors that contribute to our ability to experience empathy: genetics and socialization. Essentially, it boils down the age-old relative contributions of nature and nurture. Our parents pass down genes that contribute to our overall personality, including our propensity toward sympathy, empathy, and compassion. On the other hand, we are also socialized by our parents, our peers, our communities, and by society. How we treat others, and how we feel about others, is often a reflection of the beliefs and values that were instilled at a very young age.

A Few Reasons Why People Sometimes Lack Empathy:

We fall victim to cognitive biases: Sometimes the way we perceive the world around us is influenced by a number of cognitive biases. For example, we often attribute other people's failures to internal characteristics, while blaming our own shortcomings on external factors. These biases can make it difficult to see all the factors that contribute to a situation and make it less likely that we will be able to see a situation from the perspective of another.

We dehumanize victims: People also fall victim to the trap of thinking that people who are different from us also don't feel and behave the same as we do. This is particularly common in cases when other people are physically distant from us. When we watch reports of a disaster or conflict in a foreign land, we might be less likely to feel empathy if we think that those who are suffering are fundamentally different than we are.

We blame victims: Sometimes when another person has suffered through a terrible experience, people make the mistake of blaming the victim for his or her circumstances. How often have you heard people question what a crime victim might have done to provoke an attack? This tendency stems from our need to believe that the world is a fair and just place. If we believe that people get what they deserve and deserve what they get, it fools us into thinking that such terrible things could never happen to us.

We all have our challenges with empathy. There are a variety of emotional states we inhabit that inhibit our capacity to empathize with someone. Anything on the mad, sad, glad or scared continuum can stop us from pausing and reflecting on what it's like to be that PERSON at that TIME going through that SITUATION. Or as I shared, disgust. Granted, none of us can FULLY understand the experience of another. However, there is value in holding an INTENTION to understand, as best we can.

There are two sides to empathy, giving and receiving. When they are integrated AND there are no inner obstacles to empathy, there is no distinction. We then may have a glimpse of sweet human oneness, connected on the bridge of the heart. Investigating what's between us and empathy can guide us back to that bridge.

You can explore this yourself. Healing arts professionals also meet with empathetic challenges in our personal lives. Recall the most recent time you felt disconnected from your person. Become aware of any thoughts, images, emotions or sensations that come up when you think about UNDERSTANDING as fully as you can what your person is going through. Think about it for a moment, your person is going through something that is contributing to them to feel less than satisfactory, something that's hard for them.

What comes up for you when you think about giving your attention to understanding what it's like to be them in this situation now? When I think about what my person is going through,

I think...

I imagine...

I feel (emotion)...

I feel or sense (body)...

What is the natural automatic response to these sentences?

These responses reveal the content forming an energized knot of the conditioned self. This energized content is both your personal obstacle to empathy and your doorway to the bridge of the heart. Once you discover those obstacles, you can use what you know about acceptance and integration to address and neutralize this charged content.

What do you think the value is of holding an INTENTION to meet our person on the bridge of the heart in any given moment is? How might that intention CHANGE the dynamic in your most precious relationships?

Here's how this might look. First, get to know when your person wants and needs empathy. What are their signals? How can you tell when there is an empathy deficit? One of the biggest clues for me is I feel disconnected from them. What are your clues that your person needs your empathy?

Conversely, become more direct and assertive about letting your person know when YOU need empathy, especially if there is a disconnect between you and your person.

When you realize that you are NOT in a place of being willing or able to empathize, consider re□uesting a timeout - a time to restore your state of being where you CAN be present for your person with empathy. Begin by completing this sentence, "To reconnect with my person RIGHT NOW, I need to sacrifice... "Take note of the first three ideas that come to mind. They will be in the form of thoughts, images, emotions and/or body sensations.

Whatever comes up, that's where your practice is.

We all need empathy, some more than others. More at some times than others. Our need varies as we journey through life. It can be hidden under layers of other needs. When our need for empathy is not met, there is an added ache to the original pain. This ache can reveal a knotted tension that limits our ability to feel any bits of empathy streaming from your person.

Integrating the polarities of the need for empathy being met / the need for empathy not being met can mitigate this ache. Often this ache is knotted up with the absence of empathy in our youth. The work here is through the doorway of accepting and integrating that unique ache - addressing the triggered pain of what it feels like when our need for empathy is met, embodying this pain and integrating it with embodying what it feels like when the need for empathy is not met.

Never underestimate or be averse to giving or feeling empathy for another human being. One day that same empathetic support and energy will return to you and possibly is the glue that holds you or puts you back to together again, much like Humpty-Dumpty!

Empathy Connects Us to the Hearts of Others

We show empathy through statements such as, "I can see you are really uncomfortable about this," and "I can understand why you would be upset." We show empathy through a hug, a reassuring touch, and even through a "high five" when our empathy relates to someone's success.

Empathy is not the same emotion as sympathy. Where empathy allows us to vicariously experience and identify with other's feelings, sympathy is a feeling of pity or sorrow for the feelings of others. With empathy we feel with someone else, with sympathy we feel for someone else.

There are many theories concerning the nature versus nurture aspect of empathic development. Are some people born virtuous and some people born evil?

Dr. Paul Zak has studied the biological basis of good versus evil behavior over a number of years and has made a very interesting discovery. He found that when people feel for other people, the stress triggers the brain to release a chemical called oxytocin. Likewise, a study at Berkely concluded that a particular variant of the oxytocin receptor gene is associated with the trait of human empathy. In the study, those who had this gene variant were found to have a more empathic nature. Dr. Zak says that this study demonstrates that some people, about five percent of our population, may have a gene variant that makes them less empathic. In other words, he says, some people are more or less immune to oxytocin.

So there is scientific evidence that the goodness trait is encoded in our genes. But nature is not the only influencing factor. We may be born with the capacity to have empathy, but our ability to apply it, to care and understand, is a learned behavior.

Social psychologists say that empathetic behavior is built from the secure attachment babies develop with their parents or primary caregivers, and by modeling their parents' empathetic behavior towards them and others. Sincere empathetic behavior develops in children whose parents constantly show, teach, and reinforce it. It is a gradual emergence that occurs with the consistency and caring shown to them during the formative years of their social and emotional development. In many cases, but not all, adults who lack empathy have been victims of childhood abuse or neglect.

Those who have had extremely painful childhoods, ones that have involved emotional, sexual, or physical abuse, often lose touch with their own feelings while shutting themselves off from the pain. Their underdeveloped coping skills leave them saddled with distress, whether their own or others, and their lack of ability to experience their own pain prevents them from feeling the pain of others. As adults their elaborately built defense mechanisms block guilt and shame while also blocking their conscience. They live life through fear, threats, punishment, and isolation rather than empathy and kindness.

In many cases the opposite is true-the person over-identifies with others' pain, is overwhelmed by it, and becomes overly empathetic to the point that they absorb the feelings of everyone around them. Their internal pain and suffering is triggered when they see others in pain and suffering, therefore become preoccupied with everyone else's pain and make it their own. I did that for most of my life. Often it was to deflect my own pain but ironically it caused me to suffer more. I had very poor coping skills and my boundaries were out of whack if existent at all. I also modeled the behavior I observed as a child.

I do think that overall, my generation, a generation that relied on human interaction, a generation where families visited relatives and friends every Sunday because there was nothing else to do, is more empathetic than the generations that have followed.

In fact, an eye opening new study presented by University of Michigan researchers at an Association for psychological science annual meeting claims that college students who started school after the year 2000 have empathy levels that are 40% lower than students thirty years prior. The sharpest drop occurred in the last nine years. The study includes data from over 14,000 students.

One reason that this is happening is because students are becoming more self-oriented as their world becomes increasingly more competitive. Some say that social networking is creating a more narcissistic generation. According to lead researchers, it is harder for today's college student to empathize with others because so much of their social interactions are done through a computer or cell phone and not through real life interaction. With their friends online they can pick and choose who they will respond to and who they will tune out. That is more than likely to carry over into real life.

This is also a generation that grew up playing video games. Much of their formative years development has been influenced by input from computer generated images and violent cyber-interactions. There has to be a connection. This may partly explain the numbing of this generation.

Another point of view was presented by Christopher Lasch, a well-known American historian, moralist, and social critic, in a book he published in 1979 called, The Culture of Narcissism: American Life in an Age of Diminishing Expectations. Lasch links the prevalence of narcissism in our society to the decline of the family unit, loss of core values, and long-term social disintegration in the twentieth century.

He believed that the liberal, utopian lifestyle of the 60's gave way to a search for personal growth in the 70's. But people were unsuccessful in their attempts to find their selves. So a movement began to build a society that celebrated self-expression, self-esteem, and self-love. That's all well and good, or so it seems, but as a result of the "me" focus, more narcissism was inadvertently created. It all backfired-aggression, materialism, lack of caring for others, and shallow values have been the result.

There are certainly many of us who have not become this way-studies speak for society in general.

Today we live with constant internal and external pressures of life. On a daily basis our society faces terrorism, crime, economic crises, widespread job insecurity, war, political corruption. We see the disintegration of morality wherever we look.

As a writer, author, and inspirer I was greatly disturbed by the overwhelming success of a book (I will not promote the name except to say that it has the word "gray" in the title) based on pornography and smut. It astounds me that millions of people have read it. My publisher would have instantly rejected a manuscript of such low moral content and offensive subject matter. Where has our appreciation for □uality literature as a society gone to?

And what has happened to our legal system? It has been demonstrated time and time again that the rights of the innocent take a back seat to the rights of the offender. Our laws do very little to control criminals. In fact, it seems as if criminals control the law. If ever an empathy disorder could spur unthinkable violence to erupt in a seemingly normal person, now is the time.

Scientists have studied empathy from many approaches and together have found both physiological and psychological roots for it. Since humans are composed of body, mind, and soul, that makes perfect sense. Many things influence our behaviors.

Simon Baron-Cohen, a developmental psychopathology and autism expert, researched the genetic and environmental aspects of empathy back in the 60's. He was curious as to why some people lack empathy in their dealings with others. His book Zero Degrees of Empathy: A New Theory of Human Cruelty is an expose of his opinions, personal experiences, and findings. The object of the book is to present a way of understanding why people do bad things. Through his book he explains away the intangible concept of evil and explores a more explainable theory-the theory that there are levels of empathy and they lie within a spectrum.

Baron-Cohen says that a person's level of empathy comes from an empathy circuit lying deep within the brain. The function of this circuit determines where a person falls within the empathy spectrum. He measures a person's level of empathy by degrees, six degrees being a high functioning empathy circuit and zero degrees a low functioning one.

He classifies people who have psychopathic and narcissistic personality disorders, those who lack the ability to feel others' feelings and cannot self-regulate their treatments of others, as zero-negative.

The best and most common way that empathy is assessed, with empathy defined as "the reactions of one individual to the observed experiences of another," is through a questionnaire called The Interpersonal Reactivity Index. The questionnaire uses 5-point scales (A = does not describe me well to E = describes me very well). This scale is used to evaluate a person's perspective of his or herself.

There are four categories of assessment. The first category is Fantasy, as in the statement, "When I am reading an interesting story or novel, I imagine how I would feel if the events in the story were happening to me. The second category is Perspective-taking, as in the statement "Before criticizing somebody, I try to imagine how I would feel if I were in their place." The third category is empathetic concern, as in the statement, "When I see someone being taken advantage of, I feel kind of protective towards them." And the fourth category is personal distress, as in the statement, "When I see someone who badly needs help in an emergency, I go to pieces."

Since empathy begins with awareness of another person's feelings and receptiveness to the subtle cues that others give off, which happen to be abilities that women are naturally adept at, females generally score higher on these types of tests.

Those who have experienced the widest range of emotions and those who are most in touch with their feelings are also more able to empathize with what others feel. These people are not typically a threat to society. But there are also those who are completely devoid of empathy. These are the people that are dangers to our society. They are ticking time bombs that may explode at any time.

What to Do When Your Partner Lacks Empathy

Were you born with the ability to feel others' feelings? I was, and one of the issues that I had to face was that not everyone is empathic.

This was very confusing to me as a child. In school, I often saw children bullying and making fun of another child. The more the child cried the more fun they made of him or her. It broke my heart and I would often try to come to the child's rescue. I was deeply perplexed at how these bullying children could stand feeling the pain of the child or the animal they were hurting. Couldn't they feel the pain?

I was perplexed too with my parents, who obviously couldn't feel my pain. How was that possible? Why could I feel their pain and they couldn't feel mine? I had the same experience in my marriage and it took me many more years to understand that some people either lack the ability to feel empathy, or they shut it down so early in their lives that they have no access to it.

I tend to believe that everyone is capable of empathy, but I don't know this for sure. What I do know is that many people have learned to shut down their feelings to such an extent that they can't feel even their own feelings - and they certainly can't feel others' feelings.

It's disconcerting to discover that your partner lacks empathy. This is the situation that Georgia found herself in:

"I was recently involved with a narcissistic man who was completely unable to empathize/care or even think about my feelings and needs. Sometimes I would have to explain how his behavior was affecting me and he would eventually acknowledge he could see how I might feel, but never changed the behavior. Can someone be taught empathy or if they don't have that ability, they never will?"

Being the optimist that I am, I think it's possible for people to learn empathy, but they would have to go through an in-depth therapeutic process of reconnecting with their own feelings first, and learning to love themselves. In my experience, narcissistic people often do not think they have a problem - It's always the other person who has the problem. Because they believe they are fine and others are "messed up," they are rarely motivated to do the inner work necessary to open to their feelings and to others' feelings. They likely shut down their feelings when they were very young and they might not realize that they lack empathy.

If you are with a partner who is narcissistic and lacks empathy, don't count on this changing. You need to either accept that this person will likely never truly care about your feelings and the effect their behavior has on you, or you need to leave. Trying to change a person who currently lacks the ability to feel empathy is a waste of time and energy.

Sometimes, a highly sensitive person who shut down their feelings early in life may suddenly find themselves feeling empathy, but I've not seen this occur very often, so it's not something to count on.

One of the hardest things to deal with in a relationship is when you can see the beautiful essence of your partner, but your partner can't see his or her own essence - or yours. Many people go into relationships because they fall in love with the essence of a person, only to find out that the person's narcissistic wounded self is in charge most of the time. I've often said that we need to be able to acknowledge and tolerate a person's wounded self - putting it into perspective - in order to create a loving relationship with them. If you are attracted to someone who has narcissistic tendencies, but are unable to put their narcissism and lack of empathy into a healthy perspective,, then that person isn't for you - no matter how much you love their essence. Being in a relationship with a narcissist is never easy, and it's especially difficult for someone with empathic tendencies.

A SIMPLE EXERCISE TO READ THE EMOTIONS OF OTHERS

Restak provides a simple exercise to improve our ability to read the emotions of others based on the fact that "when a person pretends an emotion, he or she activates the same brain areas that would be activated in circumstances when the emotions are naturally and spontaneously expressed."

Start by grabbing a trusted and interested friend. Sit on the floor about 3 feet apart, and have your friend close her eyes.

Then, while gazing into her face, ask her to think about the saddest moment in her life. She shouldn't speak or otherwise respond by sighing, touching, or frowning. Study her face for the subtle changes that accompany her recall of the sad experience.

After a minute, ask her to clear her mind and think of nothing in particular. … Observe any facial changes that may occur as her thoughts shift from sad to neutral. At this point, ask your friend to open her eyes and look directly into your eyes. Ask her once again to think about her saddest experience, then of an emotionally neutral experience, and finally her happiest experience. Keep focused on her face, particularly her eyes as she shifts from one internal experience to the other. What changes do you observe?

Now shift roles.

Let your partner observe you first with your eyes closed as you think sad, indifferent, and happy thoughts. Then open your eyes and repeat the se□uence. At this point in the exercise, both of you should spend one minute mentally organizing your impressions. Then share your observations and impressions.

Here is where things get interesting. What did you observe and how does it compare to what she tells you?

Does hearing the details of what she was thinking enrich your observations in any way? While she's speaking of the sad experience, try to see once again those earlier changes in her eyes and face. Can you now detect something in her eyes or facial expression that escaped you when you were observing her a moment ago? Listen closely while she describes how you appeared to her when you were recalling the saddest and happiest moments in your life.

The most common reason the exercise fails is that as if by force of nature, we try to conceal our facial expressions.

Both of you must remain psychologically undefended, vulnerable. It's also important that during the eyes-open part of the exercise you continue to maintain firm but gentle eye contact; not the eye contact of a salesperson or an interviewer, but that of a curious child who remains relaxed and open to a new experience.

You're not trying to "stare down" your partner, but intuitively enter into and participate in his or her inner experience.

This exercise is really intense. Pick your partner carefully. You'll be dealing with subtle displays of emotion that we all have, however, unlike in social situations, you will get to test the accuracy of your emotional perceptiveness with the other person.

Chapter Three

TRAIT OF EMOTIONALLY INTELLIGENT PEOPLE

In life, we tend to live up to certain values and qualities in order to lead life rightfully and to the fullest. Little did we know some of these qualities are connected in enhancing our emotional intelligence?

Emotional intelligence is a combination of an individual's capabilities to identify, control and manage their own feelings and others' while utilizing these emotions to aid in their problem solving and get things done. The concept of emotional intelligence has been around since 1990, but only in recent years that it has been recognized as a must have soft skill in leadership and relationship building.

As many people today know, there are so many different ways to be "intelligent." Some people are book smart, others are geniuses at reading people, some are sales mavens while others have a high level of what is known as emotional intelligence. Emotional intelligence (EI) is one of those unique forms of "smarts" that helps so many people today succeed not only in their personal endeavors but in their professional lives as well.

"It is very important to understand that emotional intelligence is not the opposite of intelligence; it is not the triumph of heart over head—it is the unique intersection of both." – David Caruso

"Anyone can become angry—that is easy. But to be angry with the right person, to the right degree, at the right time, for the right purpose, and in the right way—that is not easy."

In this quote, the philosopher Aristotle perfectly sums up a concept that has become a hot topic in psychology, education, and business – emotional intelligence.

Emotionally intelligent people engage in a number of habits and behaviors that contribute to their ability to manage their own emotions and understand the feelings of others. Do you know anyone who is keenly attuned to his or her own feelings, capable of expressing emotions in an appropriate way, as well as empathetic and understanding of how others are feeling? That person is probably a very emotionally intelligent individual.

Emotional intelligence involves four major skills:
- ✓ The ability to perceive emotions
- ✓ The ability to reason with emotions
- ✓ The ability to understand emotions
- ✓ The ability to manage emotions

What is that one quality which makes some people more successful than others? Could it be simple intelligence? Maybe. However, that doesn't seem to be the whole story. According to recent studies, people of average IQ outperformed people with a high IQ.

Some say that Emotional Intelligence (EI) is a much more accurate predictor of success. Although EI is hard to define, there are some ⬜ualities that are typical of people with high Emotional Intelligence.

Check out these key things that emotionally intelligent people do so that you can try to make some of these a habit in your own day-to-day life.

Here Are Traits That People With High Emotional Intelligence Have:

Not a perfectionist

If you are emotionally intelligent, you know that perfection doesn't exist. You reject frustration and sense of failure that accompany that constant striving for perfection. If you are aware that perfectionism will leave you hung up on shortcomings of others, as well as your own, you are emotionally mature. Striving to be perfect, you may be unable to enjoy your achievements.

You know your strengths and weaknesses

If your EI is of a high level, you know how to embrace your strengths and how to use them in such a way as to compensate for your weaknesses. At work and in your social life, you will deliberately choose situations which bring out your strengths so that you can succeed. Whenever possible, you will also choose friends and co-workers who play to your strengths and help you with your weaknesses.

"Over the years, I've learned that a confident person doesn't concentrate or focus on their weaknesses – they maximize their strengths." – Joyce Meyer

Self-motivated

Your motivation comes from within and not from an external source. You do not re□uire a reward to accomplish your goals because motivation comes from you. You are clear about your goals and you do not need reminders. Emotionally intelligent people are able to set tasks for themselves and work towards them on their own.

Have empathy for others

People with high emotional intelligence have a lot of empathy. That means you should be curious and genuinely interested in other people, have the ability to tune into body language and facial expressions to understand people's emotions even without words.

Do you like asking questions to learn more about other people and their needs? If your answer is "no", hurry up and learn to summarize what people tell you. Show your understanding. If your answer is "yes", you must be an active listener which means your level of emotional intelligence is high.

You don't focus on past mistakes

If you have high EI, you realize that there is nothing to be gained from holding on to the past. You are able to remember your mistakes well enough to learn from them, but you can keep them at a sufficient distance to avoid bogging down in negative memories and experiences. You realize that regret will hold you back from fully embracing the present.

Not easily distracted

You are able to be fully present in whatever tasks you're doing. You focus on completing one task at a time and don't allow other tasks or distractions to get in the way. You recognize the difference between multitasking and multi-focusing. You will not change your goals until they are accomplished. You are not derailed from your goals by things like social media or some negative thoughts.

Work-life balance

No matter how busy you are at work or at school, to be considered an emotionally intelligent person you have to recognize the importance of sparing time for some social life. You have good time management skills and realistic ideas of how long it will take you to accomplish things. You understand that you should work very hard to achieve success, but you also know that sometimes you have to be able to disconnect completely from work duties in order to recharge.

Know when to say no

Even though saying "no" may be difficult sometimes, you should know your limits and recognize that you can't do everything. You don't give into impulses. You don't make any long-term commitments without thorough consideration first.

Emotionally intelligent people know how to give a vague response such as "maybe" or "I'll think about it" in situations that require immediate rejection. To be emotionally intelligent one should decide on priorities and be aware that by refusing some commitments you will be given a chance to fully focus on tasks you already have.

Don't fear change

Emotionally intelligent people know that fear of changes will hold them back and prevent from achieving their goals. Change is necessary for professional growth, stimulation, and success. One should always be prepared for a change that comes along, and be flexible enough to adapt whenever necessary.

When life comes to a standstill for too long, don't let it bore you. Look for some dynamic forces needed to foster creativity, life energy and that way show your emotional intelligence. Emotionally intelligent people have a positive attitude towards change and recognize that it leads to better things.

"Progress is impossible without change, and those who cannot change their minds cannot change anything."- George Bernard Shaw

They are creative thinkers.

While someone with high Emotional Intelligence might not necessarily work in a particularly creative field, they will often have a creative outlook or be the "out-of-the-box thinker" of the office. This is linked back to their overall awareness of others' emotions and their never-ending curiosity for life and the people in it. This allows them to see all of the other possible solutions available. In turn, this makes them a huge business asset.

They are hard to offend.

This is probably my favorite characteristic of people with high Emotional Intelligence. They are some of the most easygoing people you will meet. You can't easily offend them because they have a firm grasp on who they are as a person. For this reason, they are unlikely to be swayed by someone else's opinion if it contradicts with their sense of self-worth. They know who they are and they don't care about other opinions.

Know how to manage your emotions

Emotionally intelligent people are able to name their emotions and figure out why something upsets them in order to take some positive actions and improve the situation. They know that anger needs to be properly channeled and directed towards situations and events rather than people.

Approach every situation rationally keeping your emotions in check. Be confident and secure enough to not get offended over trivial things. If someone teases you about something, learn to brush it off and even laugh along with them.

If you are one of the lucky folks who have high Emotional Intelligence, congratulations! You are likely to succeed in whatever you put your mind to. If you feel that those features described above are not ☐uite peculiar to you, think about stuff you should work on. Even taking some simple steps toward self-improvement could make a big difference and reveal your self-awareness which is a constituent of Emotional Intelligence.

THE TWELVE ELEMENTS OF EMOTIONAL INTELLIGENCE

Intellect and emotional intelligence are very different things. The former is the cognitive ability to synthesize and analyze data; to problem-solve and make associations based on available information. The latter is a set of innate and learned skills which facilitate relationships and enable a person to negotiate more easily through all areas of life.

Intellect can be measured by standardized IQ tests but there is no actual measure of the "EQ," or Emotional Quotient. Even without a test, it's obvious when someone has a high IQ and it's just as obvious when someone has a high EQ. Rather than try to measure it, though, it's more useful to look at the various elements that go into emotional intelligence.

While the IQ remains stable over a person's lifetime, the EQ can be developed. Ac uiring and practicing the following elements will enable you to boost your EQ.

The first element of emotional intelligence is empathy. The ability to understand what other people are feeling will make you more sensitive and aware and will result in more meaningful relationships.

The second element is the recognition that your actions have conse uences. This understanding will enable you to make conscious choices in your life and to avoid unnecessary difficulties.

Third on the list is good judgment. The gift of making well-thought-out decisions and seeing people for who they really are will maximize the possibilities of success in all areas of your life.

Number four is personal responsibility. When you hold yourself accountable and don't blame anyone else for your mistakes or misfortunes, you are empowered to change things for the better. Other people respect you, because you own up to your part in your relationships.

The fifth element is insight. The ability to see yourself clearly and to understand your own motivations allows for the possibility of personal growth. Insight into others allows you to have a greater impact in your relationships

Element number six is mental flexibility. Being able to change your mind or to see things from different points of view makes it possible for you to navigate all sorts of relationships and to succeed where other, more rigid thinkers would fail.

The seventh element is compassion. Being honest with yourself can be painful but with a kind and gentle attitude, it's much easier. This type of compassion facilitates personal transformation, while compassion toward others supports deeper, more loving connections.

The eighth element is integrity. Following through on commitments and keeping your promises creates much good-will in personal and professional relationships and promotes success in both arenas.

Ninth on the list is impulse control. Thinking before speaking or acting gives you a chance to make deliberate, even sophisticated choices about how you present yourself to others. Not acting out of primitive impulses, urges or emotions avoids social embarrassment.

The tenth element is the ability to defer gratification. It's one thing to want something but the ability to put off having it is empowering. Mastery of your needs allows you to prioritize around life goals.

Number eleven on the list is perseverance. Sticking with something, especially when it's challenging, allows you to see it through to completion and demonstrates to others that you are dependable and potentially a high achiever.

The twelfth and final element is courage. Emotional courage (as opposed to the physical variety) is the ability to do the right thing, see the truth, open your heart and trust yourself and others enough to be vulnerable, even if all this is frightening. This causes others to hold you in high regard.

All these elements combine within you to make up your emotional intelligence. With a high EQ, even a simple person is at an advantage in life. Without it, even someone with the most brilliant intellect is at a disadvantage.

Chapter Four

EMOTIONAL INTELLIGENCE IN LEADERS

"No one cares how much you know, until they know how much you care." -theodore roosevelt

Successful leaders have many things in common, and one of the traits they share is a high degree of emotional intelligence. What that means, in a nutshell, is that they have the capacity to recognize feelings-both theirs and others'-and use that knowledge to motivate, inspire, and manage.

Many people have derailed their careers because they're deficient in emotional intelligence. While they possess the scholastic intelligence re□uired to be successful, they may fail in leadership roles if they aren't keenly aware of how their behavior and communication styles affect their colleagues and subordinates

When we look at leadership and its history, some leaders emerge with charisma, strategy, and vision as hallmarks of their style. These are absolute leadership traits, but a newer trait, called Emotional Intelligence, is making its way into leadership toolboxes as a necessity. Emotional Intelligence, or EI, is the Intelligence Quotient of social activity. Because members of today's groups, families, communities, and corporations have a great sense of independence and a need for empowerment, leaders must act in a way that promotes authority and management while allowing for participation and empowerment. An emotionally intelligent leader knows when to exercise authority, when to allow participation, and when to keep his or her ideas, feelings, and emotions private.

Emotional intelligence is a key building block to developing self-awareness and self-confidence, and it's important for leaders to have both those ☐ualities. Those who are self-aware and self-confident are able to accomplish what we expect of leaders, including:

- ✓ Building partnerships
- ✓ Collaborating
- ✓ Gaining followers
- ✓ Exuding executive presence

Leaders who are lacking in emotional intelligence will have a hard time being successful doing any of those things. Since they're not clear about the emotions driving themselves or those around them, they often make judgment calls that aren't congruent-and that can seem like they're not fulfilling their promises.

Even more significantly, the failure to be accessible and fully present-something common in those with low emotional intelligence-may come across as being unemotional or uncaring. That's the unfortunate result of failing to establish a connection, and it's a recipe for disaster for leaders.

Every time I've asked people to tell me what characteristics their best bosses have had, the list is pretty much the same:

- ✓ Supportive
- ✓ Empathetic

- ✓ Has my back
- ✓ Fair
- ✓ Authentic
- ✓ Flexible
- ✓ Inspiring
- ✓ Gives feedback
- ✓ Makes me feel involved

Similarly, the list of characteristics their worst bosses have had doesn't vary much:

- ✓ Rigid
- ✓ Insincere
- ✓ Has to be right
- ✓ Judgmental
- ✓ Doesn't listen
- ✓ Self-absorbed
- ✓ Doesn't provide positive feedback
- ✓ Takes credit
- ✓ Idolizes himself

How are those two lists related? The characteristics seen in the best bosses all re□uire emotional intelligence, while those noted on the worst bosses list reflect a decided lack of it. Those who exhibit "bad boss" behaviors are not in touch with how their actions are landing around them.

Emotional intelligence relies on the ability to act maturely in leadership situations, and not just relying on charisma, instinct, or pure knowledge. A leader with emotional intelligence can look objectively at him or her and make style adjustments that consider the environment, the group members, and the overall goal of the organization. But how can a leader practice emotionally intelligent behaviors?

One of the first ways to practice is to ask for feedback on how you've handled a situation, conversation, or conflict. Some leaders ask for opinions from colleagues, members of the group they are leading, and even superiors. With this information, a leader can see which behaviors worked - and which ones didn't. Your hindsight, armed with this information, can show you how your actions moved the organization forward - or kept it from doing so. Another way to lead with EI is to create a participative environment, as opposed to an autocratic environment. For example, if you're accustomed to making decisions alone, start meeting with your group to solicit opinions and ideas before making a decision. When you and your group become very comfortable, you can leave some decisions to the group itself.

You can also make sure everyone is self-aware, starting with yourself. In the past few years, 360-degree feedback programs have become very popular in corporate organizations. You, as a leader, are asked to rate yourself in various behaviors - and members of your group are asked to rate you in the same behaviors, as well. The comparison between self-awareness and reality can definitely make a difference in your EI. Be aware of how you handle change, as well. An emotionally intelligent leader will accept change, become aware of its benefits, and champion the change with the group. On the other hand, a leader who acts without EI may criticize the change or just insist that the group go along with it. This isn't to say that you shouldn't accept criticism of change from the group - it simply means that you can either redirect an inappropriate criticism or suggest that the person making it turns it into a constructive solution.

The further question becomes how to implement emotionally intelligent action in various areas, including personal, family, community, and corporate situations. The personal side of EI can be the most difficult - you must look at yourself and your actions. For example, if you have a disagreement with a spouse or partner, you'll have to take the focus off of your anger with the other person - and put it on your actions. How did your actions inflame the situation? What did you say that made your spouse or partner angry? Translate this scenario into a family situation: if the disagreement is with children, ask your spouse or partner for feedback on how you handled the situation. Were you angry to the point that the children actually noticed it? Another way to act with emotional intelligence in family situations is to try a participative stance. Ask the entire family to join in on decision-making and consensus. In relation to community activity, one of the most powerful actions an emotionally intelligent leader can take is to build relationships. How do the people in the group interact with each other? Who needs what from whom? Not only should you build relationships for your own benefit, but you can also build relationships in order to be a connector. You'll be remembered for creating cohesion instead of working against it.

Think for a moment about corporate leadership. All of the ways to act with emotional intelligence in other areas of your life are applicable at work - you can take a systematic approach and implement each type of action with your work group. When you do, you'll see that you □uickly rise above the crowd.

HOW EMOTIONAL INTELLIGENCE AFFECTS LEADERSHIP

James Kouzes is the Dean's Executive Professor of Leadership, Leavey School of Business, Santa Clara University and Barry Posner, PH.D. is the Dean of the Leavey School of Business at Santa Clara University. They are the co-authors of the Leadership Challenge, a seminal book on Leadership.

For over 20 years they have surveyed workers, around the globe, asking what they admired most about their leaders. From their surveys they identified four □ualities a leader must demonstrate to attract followers:

✓ Honesty
✓ Forward-looking
✓ Inspiring
✓ Competent

It is my belief that each of these four attributes are, at least partially driven by Emotional Intelligence (EI). Emotional Intelligence is a driver of behavior, good or bad and each of these four attributes are behaviors of admired leaders. Many times leadership behavior can be enhanced by good emotions or destroyed by bad emotions. A really good ☐uestion might be; How does Emotional Intelligence impact these four most admired traits of leaders?

To answer that ☐uestion, I use of the Multiple Health System's model of Emotional Intelligence, the EQi 2.0, having five major categories (Self-Perception, Self-Expression, Interpersonal, Decision Making, and Stress Management) and 15 sub-categories. Their Emotional Intelligence model was built on Ruevon Bar-On's original studies during the early years of EI and is one of the most widely used, highly validated Emotional Intelligence, self-assessments available today. How, then, does Emotional Intelligence enhance these four leadership skills:

Honesty?

I believe it is very difficult to be honest without high levels of Empathy and Social Responsibility. Empathy, the ability to recognize, understands how other feel is crucial to building trust and trust is the foundation of effective leadership. Empathy plays here because, it is difficult to be dishonest if one has a real sense of what one feels when you have been deceived. To understand how others feel when they have been deceived is a motivator to honesty and re☐uires empathy.

Social Responsibility is one's moral compass that directs our behavior toward promoting the greater good and contributing to society and other social groups. If one feels a high level of Social

Responsibility, they are more likely to be honest with others than those sensing a lower or no social responsibility.

Forward Looking?

Being a Visionary requires higher levels of Reality Testing and Optimism that likely have the greatest impact on one's ability to look forward or be a visionary. To want to see what the future holds, one needs Optimism. Few pessimists want to look forward and even if they do, what they see is not motivating to others. A sense of Optimism and an exciting future draws followers like a magnate.

But a leader needs to be realistic about what they see and communicate reality to others. Reality Testing or the ability to see things as they really are and accurately sizing up the environment, resources, and future trends to build realistic plans and goals.

Inspiring?

Being Inspirational requires higher levels of Emotional Expression and Assertiveness. Emotionally Expressive individuals can readily express emotions and convey their feelings in a way that is constructive for others. They have a unique ability to use facial expressions and body language to express emotions and are especially adept at finding ways to express emotions both positive and negative, in ways that are well received. Assertiveness is often perceived as a negative trait but, frankly it is essential to effective leadership and a big part of being inspirational. Assertiveness allows one to draw a line between passive and aggressive words and deeds. It allows one to effectively communicate goals, dreams and a future in a manner that is clear and concise.

Competent?

Competency is often thought of as more cognitive or thinking than emotional, but emotional intelligence plays a big part in being practically capable, in the eyes of others. Those who are thought of as being highly competent are often found to have higher than normal scores in Self-Actualization and Emotionally Self-Aware. Self-Actualization allows one to be aware of things that are really important in a manner that eludes to a plan. A higher score in this area indicates that you will not likely be satisfied with the status uo.

To be emotionally Self-Aware is really the beginning of understanding others. Competency in one's role demands awareness of your own emotions, as well as others. You must be Self-Aware before you can be aware of others.

To determine leadership potential and/or build on strengths and manage weakness of existing and potential leaders, I have found the measurement of Emotional Intelligence levels to be an excellent indicator of potential and a great coaching tool. In building and coaching leaders we have found that high levels of overall Emotional Intelligence and higher scores in the EQi 2.0 subscales: Empathy, Social Responsibility, Optimism, Reality Testing, Emotional Expression, Assertiveness, Self-Actualization and Emotional Self-Awareness are excellent indicators of leadership potential and provide great opportunities to coach leaders to even more productive level.

BENEFITS OF EMOTIONAL INTELLIGENCE FOR LEADERS

Businesses across a broad spectrum of industries have been helping their employees develop their Emotional Intelligence (EI) skills for more than a decade. People improving their skills have held positions ranging from the executive level to administrative staff. The one factor all these people have in common is "how they feel" or the emotions they experience despite the fact that the challenges and pressures they face at the various organizational levels are ☐uite different. Empowering people by helping them develop EI skills, enables them to become internally self-managed and capable of making their greatest contributions. And the organization itself performs best when its employees work in that zone of peak performance. The examples below explain how development of EI skills can benefit executives, high potential people and managers or supervisors.

Executives:

Executives must make decisions daily that may make or break their companies. They must rely on more people than ever to achieve results they, personally, are held accountable for by the board. Inspiring and energizing their followers, they must ☐uickly and flexibly lead system-wide organizational change. This constant, burdensome pressure can create feelings of anxiety, fear, caution, and even guilt and depression. "The Street" may hamper the company's ability to meet its goals and stockholder expectations by undervaluing the company if the executive makes a wrong decision, an untimely decision or no decision.

Research has shown that high EI skills are the distinguishing characteristics that separate star performing executives from average ones. Enhancing leaders' EI skills enables them to lead with courage, demonstrate their passion, grow and retain talented leaders, and empathize with people while humanely challenging them to meet demanding business goals. When a leader creates a flexible, resilient, strong organizational culture, he or she attracts talented people, ensuring organizational success and creating a lasting legacy.

High Potential People:

High Potential People take on demanding multiple projects and leadership roles. They may face unforeseen events that can delay or derail critical business initiatives for which they are responsible. Daily they may interact with customers, suppliers and even competitors who can be threatening and irate. Hundreds of emails demand immediate attention. These situations can cause the person to feel anxious, fearful and overwhelmed. They may feel frustrated that things are not moving faster and may worry that problems are hurting their career. Negative emotions can lead to poor decisions and multi-million dollar flubs. As critical details fall through the cracks, products flop and marketing campaigns go awry. A shallow talent pool can keep the company from developing new products and services, crippling its chances in its industry.

Since high EI skills are a distinguishing characteristic between average and high-performing individuals, then the earlier these skills are developed and ingrained, the more likely High Potentials and the company are to experience success. Ensuring that high potential people develop their EI skills to the fullest assures a cadre of competent global leaders available to introduce new products, start new businesses, and lead the integration of new acquisitions.

Managers and Supervisors:

Managers' and Supervisors' behavior and treatment of their people determine turnover and retention. They interact daily with individuals who have distinct needs, wants and expectations. They significantly influence the attitudes, performance, and satisfaction of employees within their department and other departments. The stress of trying to lead and satisfy so many people's changing needs and expectations can be overwhelming, to say nothing of the demands from upper management. Being both firm and caring at the same time causes many to feel inadequate for the role. Forty percent of turnover is reportedly due to an inadequate relationship between the employee and their direct supervisor. Where trust is lacking, performance suffers.

Enhancing EI skills enables Supervisors and Managers to regulate their emotions and motivate themselves more effectively. This allows them to manage their own emotional turmoil effectively and demonstrate compassion and empathy for their employees. EI also provides them with the courage to push against the system to make necessary changes for their people. All employees want a supportive, caring Supervisor or Manager who has their best interests at heart. Knowing this, the employee will be more likely to turn down offers from other companies to work for such a person.

Results:

While it's evident that developing EI skills can be extremely valuable to the individual and the organization, it's beneficial to examine actual results people have achieved. Program participants have reported improvements ranging from 20% to 40% reduction in stress and worry, 20% to 35% increase in personal productivity, 15% to 35% increase in teamwork, and similar improvements in personal motivation, creativity, work/life balance, management of emotional reactiveness and more. These increases can translate into positive return on investment for the organization.

How Emotional Intelligence Creates Effective Leaders

Research indicates that Emotional Intelligence (E.I.) - how we handle ourselves and our relationships - can determine success more than I.Q. In fact, E.I. may determine as much as 80% of a person's life success. Cognitive ability or what we call I.Q. is only about 20%. Quality leadership training is a combination of E.I. and cognitive ability.

More specifically, Daniel Goleman (along with two E.I. researchers: Richard Boyatzis and Annie McKee) explains the role of E.I. in leadership in Primal Leadership, Realizing the Power of Emotional Intelligence (2002). They found the most effective leadership and management styles work through emotions which evolve from the limbic system in the brain.

The limbic system is responsible for sending information to the prefrontal lobes for analysis and decisions. This system is an open-loop design which means other people can and do change our physiology by altering our hormone levels, cardiovascular function, sleep rhythms and immune function. A leader's primary task is to drive emotions in a direction which has positive impact on motivation, strategy and productivity.

Important new research clearly indicates that we rely on connections with others for our emotional stability and motivation. Who is the most likely person employees will be watching? The leader of a group has the strongest impact because people take emotional cues from the top which ripple throughout the organization's emotional climate. In addition, it is not just what another does but how it is done that registers in our limbic system.

Our emotions automatically shift to match the person we are with, even if the contact is nonverbal. This is called "entrainment" and can take place in a couple of minutes in some situations. The more cohesive the group, the more likely moods will be shared - positive or negative.

A Yale study on moods found that moods influence how effectively people work. A primary factor in how well an organization functions depends on how the leaders manage their moods. We know upbeat moods increase cooperation, fairness and business performance. Cooperative and harmonious groups reflect a higher expression of every person's best effort and ability.

Furthermore, how people feel about working at an organization (the climate) can influence productivity. Low morale and lack of cooperation predict high turnover and lower productivity. In addition, distress and worry decrease mental abilities and E.I. This makes it difficult to read the emotions of other people accurately - a skill necessary for empathy.

In addition, research indicates that the emotional state and actions of leaders set the climate. They create the conditions that determine the employees' ability to work well. In general, leaders need to be more supportive and empathetic as work becomes more emotionally demanding. When leaders are negative and unmotivated, there is anxiety and dissonance which undermines morale. When leaders are out of touch with the feelings of employees, they create dissonance. This causes people to feel off-balance, be easily distracted, and perform poorly.

In contrast, emotionally intelligent leaders create resonance or harmony. Resonant leaders rally people around a worthy goal. They are self-aware, in touch with the truth about themselves and their feelings. They use self-management to express emotions appropriately and are able to empathize with others. Without empathy, resonant leadership is impossible. When leaders are energetic and enthusiastic, an organization thrives.

The most effective leadership and management style will use a combination of Emotional Intelligence and cognitive ability. While cognitive ability tends to be set, E.I. is learned through practice, feedback and repetition over time. Although learning to improve Emotional Intelligence is self-directed, it cannot be done in isolation.

Coaching is an ideal way to provide a safe context for change to occur and to better prepare people to be resonant leaders. Some leaders find it difficult to get honest feedback as they are promoted into management positions because employees instinctively want to please their boss and are hesitant to give negative feedback. This can decrease self-awareness and effective leadership development. The coaching process provides essential feedback for continued awareness and skill building.

In summary, to effectively lead and manage relationships, leaders must continue to:

Be self-aware

Manage themselves appropriately

have empathy with their employees

Leaders need a safe space for learning and feedback which is focused on emotional and intellectual learning. Change occurs through a process which affects individuals, teams and the organization's culture. Coaching supports and enriches the process.

ATTITUDES OF EMOTIONALLY INTELLIGENT LEADERS

I had the chance to talk to my mentor and she shared with me her opinion on attitude of emotional intelligent leaders.

She stated them below;

Emotionally Intelligent Leaders and Managers get the best results!

Like learning to drive, leading and managing people are an experiential journey.

My entrance onto the leadership stage was when I was promoted into the role, having stood in for the team leader from time to time I don't know about you, but although I had practiced at managing people I hadn't experienced it properly until I had to do it for real.

Junior leaders and managers are appointed because they have shown potential, displayed leadership skills or are extremely good in the specific field they are in. More senior leaders and managers can have had a most distinguished career as a professional, i.e. doctor or lawyer or accountant, and the next step for their career is to manage people with the same specialism. An entrepreneurial business owner may be extremely successful and have ac□uired commercial business acumen and savvy long before they actually have to employ people.

So people enter leadership and management at all stages. Often their success as a leader or not; will be determined by their people skills, and if these skills haven't had a chance to develop then the most successful entrepreneur or professional may well find the going very tough indeed.

One of the most impactful people skills is emotional intelligence. Wikipedia describes emotional intelligence as" the ability to identify, assess, and control the emotions of oneself, of others, and of groups".

If you've ever been in an office where you have seen people have tantrums of a two year old, or the rumor mill is the most reliable communication channels, or there is a prevalent blame culture, then you know that emotional intelligence is somehow lacking.

Even worse, if conflict is commonplace, and your people aren't firing on all cylinders or even are openly disengaged then you have may have a problem which stems from limited or unrecognized poor emotional intelligence.

Depending on our psychological profile, and we are all thankfully different; then you may have brilliant emotional intelligence, or conversely you may need to develop this skill more. The great thing about emotional intelligence is that if you are struggling, you can learn!

My first challenge as a young manager was learning how to control my own emotions. In the early years I was □uite often daunted about having to deal with some larger than life characters I had to manage. Managing my fear was one of my first and probably my longest lessons. I still feel afraid sometimes, but now I know how to deal with it, and it doesn't faze me.

My second challenge was to learn how to manage the emotions of my team. This stage was a long one and a steep learning curve. The journey was interesting, thought provoking and a necessary one.

The final stage in my learning came when I had to think about engaging large teams. Some of who I didn't see for months at a time. Although I did try to do the best I could to have physical contact as much as I could humanly manage. Trying to encourage people to feel good, fulfill their potential and understand how much I appreciated them was more difficult. Although there are many skills attached to managing remotely, my own emotional intelligence was a key player in making remote management a success.

I have worked for and supported many managers and managed teams locally, regionally and nationally. During this time I have practiced and observed attitudes and behaviors which have been the most successful in getting the best out of a team. These attitudes and behaviors are most commonly adopted by people who have honed their emotional intelligence skills and have the best people skills as a result. I have practiced these in the latter years, and wished I had access to and learned them in the early years.

The Nine Attitudes are:

Accepting people completely for who they are

Always looking for the good in people, there is always some

Dealing with negatives in an impersonal but practical way and getting over it!

Not judging - we all make mistakes.

Giving people the benefit of the doubt

Listening to what people need and wherever possible - obliging

Responding neutrally to anger or other attacking behavior and helping the person to reframe it in a positive way.

Pivoting negative situations to achieve a positive outcome.

Caring about people, even when they were difficult.

You might be thinking that it all sounds unrealistic, given some of the people you might be managing. But I can guarantee that if you think about it enough, they are all attitudes or stances you would like people to take with you.

Unfortunately we aren't born with an instruction manual and so navigating and improving our own emotional intelligence often comes through our own life experiences and self-reflection. However the good news is that there are some clear and easy steps to improving our own emotional intelligence and therefore that of your team and organization.

Emotional Intelligence - 3 Tips For Leadership Success

When people are asked what traits and □ualities they admire in their mentors and leaders, the typical responses are that they are caring, engaging, authentic, positive thinkers, creative, patient, empathetic, charismatic and thoughtful. These □ualities are not taught in college textbooks or graduate school courses. They are learned and developed by people who have come to understand the value of Emotional Intelligence.

In our competitive business world, Emotional Intelligence, or EQ, is more important than your IQ. Your ability to connect with people on a genuine human level and build rapport with them is essential if you want to climb the ladder of success, and stay at the top.

Regardless of where you went to college and your SAT scores, your IQ can not be changed. The number you were born with is yours for life. IQ measures spatial and cognitive reasoning and is mathematically-based. It can help you in solving right angle problems and theorems but will not help in resolving breakdowns in communication while planning a team retreat, budget meeting or website overhaul. While education is so important in the building of our foundations and disciplines, a degree from an Ivy League school and an impressive IQ do not ensure that you have ade□uate communication skills to connect with others and be successful in the workplace.

Emotional Intelligence is what I call "street smarts." EQ is a huge factor in communication and conflict resolution, both at work and home. Individuals with high levels of EQ have compassion, empathy, congeniality, patience, assertiveness and self-awareness. Again, the good news is that EQ can be learned.

According to a survey conducted by U.S. News & World Report, 90% of people are fired from their jobs because of attitudinal or relationship problems. Only ten percent lose their jobs due to lack of skills or ability. A huge part of our success is based on our attitudes, communication and mindsets.

Developing Emotional Intelligence comes with age. Allow me to get scientific for just a moment. EQ is directly linked to our brain functions. The amygdala part of our brains is responsible for pulling out emotional meaning from nonverbal messages, like a scowl, shifts in posture and eye contact. The amygdala reads the emotional aspect of whatever we perceive. The problem is that this portion of our brain is not fully developed until the age of 25. This is why older people tend to be more adept at managing a variety of emotions and reactions. Chalk it up to life's experiences.

Top leaders understand that they need to be aware of how they behave, react, and respond in stressful situations and conflicts. It's important to know the "triggers" that can potentially set you off.

In the leadership training programs I provide on Emotional Intelligence and Neurolinguistic Programming (NLP), I repeatedly hear scenarios from people about how they mishandled situations with colleagues, clients and prospects. Examples include raising voices, interrupting, criticism, defensive tone of voice, and negative body language.

Here are 3 Tips to Improving Your Emotional Intelligence:

1. Start watching people. Identify a few people who you admire for their empathy, self-confidence and assertive communication. Observe how they interact with others. Be aware of how people with strong Emotional Intelligence handle difficult people and situations. Leaders with high levels of EQ tend to bring individuals together instead of dividing them. They are able to articulate and convey their opinions, recommendations, feelings and thoughts in a confident and calm way that is considerate and respectful to everyone. They don't blame others. They take full responsibility for their actions and behavior.

2. Develop assertive communication skills. People who lead and live with EQ understand that every spoken sentence does not re□uire an answer. They don't react and they definitely don't over-react. Silence may initially feel awkward but silence is conversations and in conflicts can be extremely powerful. By asking good □uestions and truly listening, leaders show others that they genuinely care and are empathetic. Practice with the approach of less talking and more listening.

3. Validate the other person's feelings. Avoid shifting the focus of the conversation. It's important to allow others to express themselves without judging, criticizing or interrupting. If a co-worker complains to you that their items in the budget were cut, allow them to vent for a few minutes. Don't spend too much time talking about how you felt when you fell victim to a budget crunch at your old job. Even if you have never experienced the swinging budget ax, you can still be compassionate and listen. You don't have to fall out of a window to know it hurts.

Management and business guru Jim Rohn said, "Work on your career and you'll make a living. Work on yourself and you'll make a fortune.

Chapter Five

EMOTIONAL INTELLIGENCE IN THE WORKPLACE

Many individuals have tried to incorporate concepts of emotional intelligence within their business settings. However, few organizations have changed for the better. Therefore, an error or misapplication of those principles must have interfered. An emotionally intelligent organization represents an environment which efficiently and successfully adapts to changes and achieves its goals, managing simultaneously to be responsible and sensitive to its personnel, customers, suppliers, networks and society. Such an organization is very popular in the competition "The Best Companies to Work For".

Google is a suggestive example as they hire people that excel not only in technical expertise but also in emotional intelligence skills such as assertiveness, independence and interpersonal relationship skills. The persons endowed with such capacities have a better management of themselves and re□uire less training and supervision to get a job done. Not to mention that they encourage their managers to take risks, which altogether generates an engaged workforce?

There are several factors that must be considered in order to achieve emotional intelligence in the workplace. These are: the people, the work and the purpose. Each of them involves numerous aspects. Let us study them separately.

When tackling with personnel, employers have to make sure they are:

Hiring the right persons: having both technical and emotional intelligence skills;

Designating the right people to the right tasks: a better performance is obtained by matching EI skills to the right job;

Encouraging and using to the fullest supportive co-workers;

Creating and nurturing an environment of cooperation, socializing and development of friendships;

Training supervisors and managers: these positions have to be filled by persons that have interpersonal skills, not only technical knowledge.

As far as the factor of work is concerned, an emotionally intelligent job implies:

Challenging tasks that stimulate motivation and a greater degree of engagement;

The appropriate resources and e□uipment;

Fair compensations;

Tasks that are neither over- or under-soliciting.

The third factor, the purpose, is very important in the satisfaction of the employees. They perceive a reason for their work if:

Their work brings contributions to the community, society, country or world;

They are aware of what the company stands for.

Over the past two decades, we have seen our HR roles change from being primarily administrative to making strategic decisions regarding our company's future direction. A key component of this new role is identifying and strategically aligning our talent. The importance of this responsibility cannot be stressed enough, but how do we go about finding the right people?

In the past, new hires and promotions were based on technical ability or the candidate's education and experience. If someone had the needed skills and experience, it was assumed that they would make good leaders and be able to pass their knowledge along to others. Sometimes that held true, but we all know that it is possible for an employee to have the necessary degrees, be an absolute wiz at his job and still "be a cancer within the company."

Let's talk about Carl. Carl is a fantastic employee. His numbers are always at the top of the list. He's worked for you for years. He never takes a sick day and is never late. He often works late into the night just to get things done. Carl is dedicated and driven. However, Carl is a hard charger, and no one can stand to be around him.

Carl is not going to win any popularity contests. No one goes to lunch with Carl. His management style is one of intimidation and insult. He is arrogant and abusive. He browbeats those who work under him. It seems that Carl does not know how to get his message across without an insult. He holds himself to a high standard, and he cannot fathom those who do not hold themselves to the same standard.

He does not understand that he is part of the problem. When people are assigned to Carl's team, their numbers inevitably go down. Carl turns a good employee with good productivity into someone who no longer wants to come to work. Carl is a poison, but what do you do about Carl?

How did Carl rise through the ranks of your company if he is such a poor leader and communicator? That is easy. He was very good at his job. Many companies promote based on performance with little regard to the soft skills that make someone a stronger leader. In fact, Carl's poor habits have been reinforced. After all, he keeps being promoted. He must be doing everything right.

When results are all that matter, you get results oriented employees whose methods may not be sustainable or scalable. In the 1990's, Dr. Daniel Goleman introduced a new way of predicting success. Rather than focus on technical ability or IQ, as the sole predictor of success, he advocates focusing on Emotional Intelligence (EI).

Emotional Intelligence focuses on four key factors that successful leaders must have: Perceiving Emotions, Emotional Reasoning, Understanding Emotions, and Managing Emotions.

Perceiving Emotions- This is one's ability to recognize emotions in others. It involves reading others and understanding their verbal and nonverbal cues.

Reasoning with Emotions- This factor involves one's ability to choose what to pay attention to and what to ignore.

Understanding Emotions- This involves understanding what drives an emotional response in others, as well as yourself. What makes people tick?

Managing Emotions- This may be the most important aspect of Emotional Intelligence. It involves using emotions in yourself and others to attain the desired goal. People are emotional creatures. Knowing how to use those emotions to achieve positive results is a large part of being a successful leader.

Since its introduction into the business world, the effect of Emotional Intelligence has been tested in clinical and real world settings. Each time it has passed with flying colors. Employees who possess a high EI affect those around them in a positive rather than negative way, and make better employees. Companies with a large number of emotionally intelligent employees are more successful than companies with a comparatively low number of emotionally intelligent employees.

This does not mean that companies should engage in hug therapy each morning. It has been proven that employees with a high EI also possess greater technical ability. They use their abilities, and the abilities of others, more effectively than those with a low EI. It is possible to still focus on technical ability, but include EI when it comes time to hire, fire, and promote.

Okay, Emotional Intelligence is great, and you need more high EI employees. How do you go about achieving that goal? Setting that goal is the first and most important step, and here are a few ways that you can quickly implement EI into your existing company structure.

Hire People that Possess High EI

The easiest way to change the culture of your company is through new hires. There will always be turnover in a successful company that can be viewed as an opportunity to improve the company culture. During the interview process, you can focus on hiring new employees that possess a high EI.

There are several ways to accomplish this, and they all rely heavily on the interview process. At the beginning, there is no reason to retain experts on EI or conduct an extensive battery of tests. A simple shift of focus from work related experience to Emotional Intelligence during the interview process is a strong step in the right direction. Use the interview to examine a candidate's emotional response to stressful situations. Make certain that the candidate is being specific. Do not let them get by with just a general response.

Assess Your Current Employees

Hiring is one way to increase the Emotional Intelligence of your company, but you cannot simply terminate everyone and start from scratch. Your company already has a staff in place. This means assessing your employees with an eye toward EI. Several tests that measure EI are available.

The instrument is not as important as the act of measuring and expecting EI. The act itself will send the message that this is now important within your company. It will also help you identify those who may be suited for a larger role within your company.

Stress How Results are Obtained Rather than the Results Themselves

Results are relevant. You want your employees to perform well, but the methods they employ to achieve those results are also essential. Your employees need to know this. Make sure that you are stressing the importance of communication, teamwork, and flexibility when performing your assessments.

Promote the Right People

When it comes time to fill a position within the company through promotion, make sure that you promote people who demonstrate a high level of EI. Before promoting, you should ask the candidates pointed questions about what they think it takes to be effective in their new position. Then, ask them how they have demonstrated those skills in their current positions. Once again, by stressing EI in the promotion process, you are sending a message to the rest of your company that these are valuable traits.

Okay, you know how to implement EI into your company's HR practices, but is it worth the trouble? Not every employee is like Carl, and you have been doing pretty well over the years. What results can you expect to see if you implement these changes? Let's look at some hard numbers.

Credit card giant American Express integrated EI into their training sessions. Employees that received training in EI saw a 20-percent increase in sales over the control group.

The United States Air Force decided to assess EI when determining which servicemen would make effective recruiters. Those with high EI were 300% more successful than their counterparts.

L'Oreal Cosmetics began to select their agents based on EI rather than on technical ability alone. In the first year, these agents outsold their counterparts by an average of over $90,000.

Emotional Intelligence is a predictor of success. No matter what business you are involved in, focusing on emotional intelligence as well as technical ability will help your company grow. Employee productivity will be better, and employee retention will increase. A business with a high EI rate is a great place to work, and talented employees will not want to leave. Companies that retain high-performing employees are successful.

EMOTIONAL INTELLIGENCE IN THE WORKPLACE - HOW DO YOU MEASURE UP?

Four factors are paramount in defining a person's emotional intelligence. These factors can strongly affect your performance at work, how much you enjoy the work you do and how you affect the environment and the people around you.

1. Social Responsibility

In the world of work, we live with other people, people with as many problems and challenges as we do, and who are dealing with them as best they can, just as we are. So when negative things happen at work because of someone else's actions, we can either take it personally and lash out in anger, or try to understand the other person's point of view and respond accordingly.

The latter course helps correct the situation instead of placing the blame, and is the choice of people of high emotional intelligence.

2. Interpersonal Relationships

Are you a giver or a taker? When takers some into conflict, there's no compromise and very little chance of resolution.

Givers rarely come into conflict with one another, but can find themselves in conflict with takers. The taker will take advantage of the finer instincts of the giver, and over time resentment will fester.

Learn to recognize the signs in yourself and those who report to you. If you have control over hiring, hire more giving people. If you have inherited a group of takers, use your communication skills to help them understand and learn to care about the conse□uences of their attitude.

3. Stress Tolerance

You already have a built-in capacity to deal with stress and anxiety, but you can also do a number of things to increase your stress tolerance level.

Learn to recognize the signals in yourself that will let you know when you are about to "lose it" □ such as your hands turning into fists or your teeth starting to clench □ in time to reverse the reaction. This will help you do some deep breathing or whatever other calming techni□ues work to reduce your personal stress level.

4. Impulse Control

People with low impulse control can be derailed by e-mail messages, meetings and other situations that can tempt them to react instinctively without engaging their critical thinking mechanism.

People with high emotional intelligence are able to delay their actions or comments until they can be made from a place of intellectual control instead of emotional reaction.

Your emotional intelligence has a huge effect on how you work, how much personal satisfaction you can have in that work and how you contribute to the environment around you.

THE EFFECTS OF LOW EMOTIONAL INTELLIGENCE IN THE WORKPLACE

Low EI can be exhibited in several ways. One of the characteristics of low EI is poor impulse control - the inability to stop, think and decide. Poor impulse control can be evidenced in an employee who reacts to situations without adequate consideration instead of planning and preparing for various scenarios. Low EI also causes difficulty managing stressful situations. There are often instances at work that induce stress, and the inability of employees to react in a mature and productive manner could severely damage an organization. Consider the following scenario:

An employee made a bid for a work project and was awarded the assignment. Work begins but the employee begins to feel overwhelmed and no longer desires to complete the project. In a panic, they return the assignment to the manager and re□uest personal time off of work.

This employee has a low Emotional Intelligence. They also displayed an inability to self-analyses to determine if they were capable of completing the project. They bid on a job impulsively without studying all the circumstances. When in a stressful situation, they chose to react hastily without considering the consequences - positive or negative - of their actions.

This type of occurrence can be extremely costly to a business. It could cause loss of clientele, personnel, time and money to reassign the project and meet client specifications.

Low levels of EI also contribute to poor emotional understanding and irrational thinking. Emotions cannot be controlled if they are not first accepted and understood. Under these circumstances employees are not able to view a situation accurately, and particularly not in relation to how it affects others.

Consider this situation:

Two employees are approaching a project deadline, and believe they may not complete the job successfully in the remaining time allotted. They continue to work on the project - missing the deadline - and then turn it in when completed. They did not provide any notice to their superior or to the client.

In this scenario, low EI has again caused the employees to react to situations from an immature view point. They realized they would not meet the deadline, but did not think further about the ramifications for the company. Nor did they seek assistance outside of themselves in order to achieve a successful outcome. Not only would this situation cost the company money, but imagine the work environment that exists if employees do not exhibit concern for their superiors. Interpersonal relationships are guaranteed to be imbalanced and unhealthy.

To correct the effects of low EI in the workplace Cognitive Behavioral Coaching (CBC) has become an increasingly popular practice in businesses. Coaching employees toward Emotional Intelligence through a deep self-awareness that examines beliefs and influences actions reverts the focus of the company from correction to production.

TIPS ON IMPROVING EMOTIONAL INTELLIGENCE AT WORK

Emotional intelligence at work is often overlooked by top management and might be the least priority in hiring company personnel. But nowadays, there is a growing need for employees to cope with work-related stress. Emotional intelligence will greatly help in achieving this. The bottom line is that when employees are coping well with the daily stresses and needs of the job, they can perform better, and this is the ultimate goal.

Ways to Improve Emotional Intelligence in the Workplace

Build Strong Relationships - From your first day of work, start forging a relationship with people you work with. Do not judge the people by their rank or title, but be open and build a support group in the workplace. These friendships or alliances can help you in achieving your goals and in performing better in the company.

Put on a Positive Attitude - A positive attitude towards work is very evident and can be contagious. When your superiors see you working with a positive attitude even when there are evident challenges, the rewards will also be forthcoming. If there are no rewards, your positive attitude can help you overcome the feeling of being unappreciated or slighted.

Controlling Emotions - People who cannot control their emotions - such as anger or jealousy - are so focused on the negative aspects that they do not realize that no one wants to side with them anymore. This prevents them from performing their job well. There is no one to support them. Work smart and be mindful of your strong emotions. Do not let them cloud your work judgment.

Avoid Blaming Others - There will always be the blame game in the workplace. This is how some people make excuses for their own mistakes and how they avoid taking responsibility for their actions. If you are the one who is responsible for a mistake, take accountability and make plans for taking action to correct the mistake. This is how you develop management and leadership skills.

The happiness of people in the workplace is so elusive for some people. Negative feelings are dominant and employees often complain about anything under the sun - from minor things like office supplies to serious matters like bad bosses and mismanagement. Negative emotions such as jealousy, envy, anger, helplessness, fear, insecurity, isolation, resentment, and feelings of being unappreciated or slighted are all contributing to how people perform their jobs.

Helping employees deal with changes and stresses will minimize these negative feelings and can lead to better performance. More importantly, it can promote the following among them: team work, leadership, best practices, and high level management skills

Chapter Six

EMOTIONAL INTELLIGENCE IN RELATIONSHIPS

Emotional Intelligence (EI) is the ability within a person to control and perceive emotions. It therefore happens to play an extremely important role in the relationships, one makes and breaks, during the course of his lifetime.

Relationships may develop when two people find each other interesting, have something in common or just enjoy each other's company. For a relationship to be strong and last longer there has to be some level of emotional attachment between those in that particular relationship. It can be observed in daily life with ease that those relationships without any emotional attachment and understanding and those with stakes, cease to exist. Understanding is therefore vital in any relationship. This comes with emotional intelligence.

With emotional intelligence, a person can understand the other and he can perceive his emotions and feelings. In every instant, he would know what to say and what to do which would bring up the morale of the other person and not make him disappointed or sad. If things go wrong, the persoN would know how to react and resolve thing in a way that nobody gets hurt.

Communication, too, is e□ually important in long-lasting relationships. Communication does not only refer to speaking. It does not only mean to say the right things at the right times, but also to stay silent and listen to the other person when need be. A good communicator will judge the mood and emotions of the other person and act accordingly, bringing emotional intelligence into play. Somebody with a high emotional intelligence will always have an edge in his personal relationships compared to a person with lower emotional intelligence. A good level of communication determines how the relationship will continue and for how long. In every relationship, whether it is friendship or marriage, communication is critical, not to mention the importance of communication in business organizations.

Patience and managing stress well help a relationship work for longer. As when one person is not happy with the way things are going the other, understanding how he might be feeling should act accordingly and help him come out of that situation for a better and stronger relationship.

In fact, if people in relationships do not have emotional intelligence, their relationship would not last too long and it would be very dry. They would not understand each other on any matter. The person would be without any feelings for the other and without any sense of keeping relationships.

EMOTIONALLY INTELLIGENT CONVERSATIONS FOR IMPROVING RELATIONSHIPS

What is a difficult conversation?
What is EQ?

How can we improve EQ?

How can EQ get us to a win-win with our difficult conversations?

What is a difficult conversation?

A difficult conversation:

Wife: I told you to leave your clothes there; you never listen to me?

Me: I told you that I do not understand there; where is there?

Wife: Now you are unnecessarily arguing, you know where there is.

Me: Sorry Madam, but your there changes everyday, so where is there today.

Wife: Why do you have to always argue and find fault with me?

Me: What is always? How many counts do you have of me arguing in the last week?

Wife: Why do I always have to be wrong?

And on and on and on, till one or the other walks off.

What is happening here? How do simple conversations become difficult?

All of us intuitively know when we are about to have a difficult conversation or when a conversation becomes difficult, including when it is about to become difficult. Yet, there are very few of us who do not have difficult conversations almost every day of our life with our significant others, whether at work, at home or at play. Usually a difficult conversation means happens when we share (give and/or receive) negative feedback with anyone. That anyone may be a boss, spouse, good friend, child, colleague or someone we love and admire and care for. Some conversations can also seem difficult because we think that we have a lot at stake or we have already taken a position which we feel a retraction will lead to loss of face. Conversations also become difficult due to our past conditioning - we expect it to be difficult because it has been so in the past. We deal with conversations in a routine manner without stopping to reflect.

Reflection questions for a difficult conversation:

1. Why do I want to have this conversation? (Self-awareness)

2. What will happen by not having this conversation? What will happen by having this conversation? (Emotional maturity)

3. What am I afraid of? What is the worst possible outcome? What is my stake? What do I expect - the best outcome? (Self-motivation)

4. What untested assumptions and inferences am I making? How can I step into the space of the other person to test my assumptions and inferences so that I can understand all perspectives with equanimity? (Empathy and Understanding)

5. Can I make a commitment to listen and understand and communicate that understanding? Can I just listen and not make any proposition until I have fully understood the other and have a confirmation to that effect? (Quality communication)

How to use EQ in difficult conversations?

We can develop some general principles on how to have difficult conversations where EQ plays a very large role for the conversations to be win-win for both parties.

1. Clarify your own purpose and intent.

The EQ ☐ualities of self-awareness and emotional maturity can help us to clarify our purpose and intent. Ask yourself why you wish to have this conversation? If your intention is unilateral - to have someone agree or support you - you are likely to have a very defensive response. If you really wish to move forward, you may enter the conversation with curiosity to explore the situation and verify the accuracy of your views. Knowing your own purpose and intent will help you to learn how to productively change your own behavior before having an impact on the other. Self-awareness helps you to clarify your intent and purpose.

Each difficult conversation is really about three things: what really happened, how you feel about what happened, and what the situation says about your identity. Get in touch with your thinking and feelings to know your fears and what your hot button issues are. This will help you to test your assumptions and attributions and validate your data. Some ☐uestions to test your emotional maturity:

Am I being compassionate towards all?

Am I open and curious or do I come with preconceived ideas? Am I willing to learn?

Am I being transparent in sharing all I know?

Am I fully committed to the outcome?

What are my worst fears? What are my deepest desires?

Am I holding myself accountable for my contributions?

2. Build a foundation for the conversation

Agree with the other person on the purpose of the conversation - what is it that you want to talk about? What is your interest in bringing about this conversation? Without this the other person is often more likely to stick with their own inferences and become defensive thereby not allowing you to make your proposition. Self-motivation is the quality that is most likely to help you as you know that you are having this conversation as a matter of choice - even though it is difficult. By using the qualities of empathy and understanding you can make the other person realize that this is not just a unilateral conversation but needs to be jointly discussed for mutual benefit. You can build the foundation in the four steps of:

Don't just say what you think happened also ask for the others view of what they think happened.

Talk about how the other feels and then share how you feel

Proposition your interests after clarifying the others needs and interests

Don't advocate solutions, ask for inputs to jointly design solutions

3. Stay focused on jointly designed process

Normally in difficult conversations we tend to go back to the history of the situation and lose track of the future goals as jointly designed. This will again re□uire self-awareness and emotional maturity to be authentic, to realize where the process is getting derailed and to focus on the process. It will also require self-motivation to continue to the end of the process. Old data is often flawed as our reasoning is faulty when we are fearful of a situation or frustrated about a relationship. Self-motivated focus will help us to stay in the present and continue towards progress in the future.

4. Agree to monitor progress and discuss again

Success in difficult situations is achieved when both do something different. As this is about changing behavior it is needed to fine-tune intentions with actions. Always agree to monitor progress and celebrate success at the end of difficult conversations.

Emotional intelligence is a factor that is just as important as home as it is at work. Your relationships will prosper when you can understand the feelings of those around you. All it takes is a little forethought and understanding.

Chapter Seven

HOW TO MEASURE YOUR EMOTIONAL INTELLIGENCE

Perhaps you may have heard that what is even more important than a person's 'IQ' is their 'EQ', or emotional intelligence, and are interested in learning more. Emotional Intelligence involves, broadly speaking, the capacity to understand and manage emotion. Can this be measured?

IQ tests are well-known assessments of cognitive capacity; however, the picture when it comes to emotional intelligence is more complicated. There are many free quizzes readily available to test EQ, but as is explained shortly, such self-report measures are not always accurate.

Ability tests of EQ fare better. In the following article, the 'ins and outs' of emotional intelligence testing are explored in some detail. Along with a rich assortment of information, this article will also provide links to some free EQ assessments and samples of questions so that you can really get a feel for EQ tests.

What is an Emotional Intelligence Test?

So, just what is a test of emotional intelligence?

Well, put simply, as opposed to a self-report scale of EI, an EI test is developed differently. You see, EI tests are based on the premise that EI consists of a group of skills that are employed in order to solve emotional problems.

Therefore, as explained by pioneers in the research area of EI, Mayer, Caruso, Salovey & Sitarenios (2003), because it is developed from a skill-base, that EI is therefore a distinct ability that can be measured objectively.

What is an EQ appraisal?

Another way of looking at the assessment of EI is an EQ appraisal. One example of an EQ appraisal is the Emotional Intelligence Appraisal that features in the best-selling work 'Emotional Intelligence 2.0' (Bradberry & Su, 2006). The appraisal was created in 2001 by Dr. Travis Bradberry and Dr. Jean Greaves and it may be administered in either online form or in a booklet. You can find more emotional intelligence books here.

The EQ appraisal is a skill-based assessment based on Daniel Goleman's four-factor taxonomy (Bradberry & Su, 2006). According to Goleman, EI consists of four components:

✓ Self-awareness,
✓ Self-management,
✓ Social awareness and
✓ Relationship management.

The EQ appraisal consists of 28 items and is performance based – it is designed to assess the behavior linked to EI skills. The assessment gives an overall EQ score, and a score for each of the four EI factors (Bradberry & Su, 2006).

Research with The Emotional Intelligence Appraisal has found Cronbach alpha reliability ratings between .85 and .91 however, interestingly, a non-significant positive correlation was found between the appraisal and the popular EI test, the Mayer-Salovey-Caruso Emotional Intelligence Test.

In the following sections of this article, you can certainly read more about the MSCEIT. Briefly, however, for the purpose of an introduction to this discussion, the MSCEIT is an ability model of EI.

Researchers have suggested that there is a distinction between the constructs that are measured by the MSCEIT and EI Appraisal (Bradberry & Su, 2006). It was reasoned that this difference in models from which the assessments were developed – the MSCEIT is an ability-based assessment, whereas the EI Appraisal was based on Daniel Goleman's 'mixed' model of EI.

It has been claimed that scores on the Emotional Intelligence Appraisal predicted job performance more than the MSCEIT, and what's more, it also takes one-fifth of the length of time to administer.

The Emotional Intelligence 2.0 Test

In this section, I will be focusing on the Mayer-Salovey-Caruso Emotional Intelligence Test, Version 2.0 (MSCEIT, V 2.0). The MSCEIT is a 141 scale that measures the four branches of EI, each branch reflecting specific skills – perceiving emotions, using emotions to facilitate thought, understanding emotions and managing emotions (Mayer, Caruso, Salovey & Sitarenios, 2003).

Each of these four 'branches' is measured in the MSCEIT using two tasks, as described below:

Branch one – perceiving emotions: faces and pictures tasks

Branch two – facilitating thought: sensations and facilitation tasks

Branch three – understanding emotions: blends and changes tasks

Branch four – managing emotions: emotion management and emotional relationships tasks.

Each of these 8 tasks is measured either by a discrete, single item or a group of individual items that make up an 'item parcel' (Mayer et al., 2003). Item parcels are collections of related items – so, for example, the 'faces task' consists of four item parcels, each containing five responses. Some items only re□uire one response per stimulus so are distinct and free-standing (Mayer et al., 2003).

Across the 8 tasks, the responses required take different forms. The test was designed this way so that the results across the response methods can be generalized, and also minimize the associated error in measurement (Mayer et al., 2003). So, some tasks use a 5-point rating scale, whereas others re□uire a multiple-choice response.

Let's look at this test a little closer…

The 'faces' task is made up of 4 item parcels, each with 5 responses (Mayer et al., 2003). In this task, participants are presented with a group of faces, and they are required to respond with the specific emotion they can identify as portrayed in the face (Mayer et al., 2003).

The 'pictures' task consists of six parcels each with 5 responses. It is similar to the 'faces' task, except that the target stimuli are abstract designs and landscapes, and to respond, participants select from cartoon faces that show specific emotions (Mayer et al., 2003).

The 'sensations' task consists of five parcels, each with three responses. Participants match sensations to the emotions they generate – e.g. describing how 'hot' or 'cold' a feeling of envy is (Mayer et al., 2003).

The 'facilitation' task is made up of 5 item parcels, each with three responses. This task re□uires a decision about the moods that are most closely associated with specific behaviors and cognitive tasks, in terms of accompanying them or assisting them. The example given by Mayer, Caruso, Salovey, and Sitanerios (2003) is "whether joy may assist planning a party" (p. 99).

The 'blends' task consists of 12 free-standing items. Responders choose which emotions could be combined to produce another emotion – for example, that malice could be formed by combining envy and aggression (Mayer et al., 2003).

The 'changes' task is made up of 20 free-standing items in which individuals choose the emotion that emerges due to another emotion intensifying – e.g. that depression is most likely to result from intensification of sadness and fatigue (Mayer et al., 2003).

The 'emotion management' task consists of 5 parcels, each with 4 responses. In this task, responders are re□uired to form a judgment about the best actions that can be taken by an individual in a story in order to result in the specified emotional outcome (Mayer et al., 2003). So, for example, the participant might read a story about a character and need to identify what this character can do to reduce their anger or prolong joy (Mayer et al., 2003).

Finally, the 'emotional relationship' task. This task is made up of 3 item parcels, each with 3 responses. This task requires test-takers to decide what are the most effective actions an individual can take in order to manage another person's feelings (Mayer et al., 2003).

Putting this all together, it can be seen that the MSCEIT 2.0 is a comprehensive test of EI. In fact, it requires a total of 705 responses – 141 items are included, each with 5 responses (Mayer et al., 2003).

Can EI Really be Measured With a Quiz?

According to Matthews, Roberts, and Zeidner (2004), there are a number of problems and serious omissions in the area of EI as measured by a simple self-report assessment.

In actual fact, this issue is what led Mayer, Caruso, and Salovey to argue that performance-based measures are needed for EI to be understood as an actual cognitive ability (Matthews, Roberts & Zeidner, 2004).

Their argument then resulted in the development of the Multi-Factor Emotional Intelligence Scale (the MEIS) and, more recently, the MSCEIT.

To consider EI as a scientific construct, it is necessary to determine whether EI is a measurable phenomenon (Matthews et al., 2004). Self-report measures of EI have shown satisfactory internal consistency reliably across a variety of cultures, as well as more than ade□uate levels of test-retest reliability over 1 – and 4-month periods (Matthews et al., 2004).

On the other hand, performance-based measures of EI have been shown to present a number of problems in terms of reliability (Matthews et al., 2004). All these issues seem to suggest that EI may not be able to be measured.

Indeed. Whether or not EI tests actually measure a theoretical construct or trait is termed 'construct validity', and, in actual fact, Matthews and colleagues (2004) concluded that neither performance-based nor self-report measures of EI meet the criteria for what is deemed 'construct validity'.

However, past research has found a relatively modest association between self-report measures of EI and actual ability measures (Matthews et al., 2004). What a complicated picture EI presents! What are we to make of these claims?

Well, further research into the measurement of EI is certainly warranted – particularly into validation studies of self-report measures of EI. According to Matthews et al (2004), "there are major conceptual, psychometric, and applied problems and issues to be overcome before EI can be considered a genuine, scientifically validated construct with real-life practical significance" (p. 192).

Other research, however, argues against what Matthews and colleagues presented in the 2004 paper titled 'Seven myths about emotional intelligence'. It does in actual fact support the notion that EI can be readily measured using tests, particularity self-report tests.

However, just because something is easily measured this does not mean that such measures are accurate.

The fact that EI is made up of a range of skills does mean that self-report is not the most accurate way to measure EI (Matthews et al., 2004). This also means, however, that even though self-report measures are not effective measures of EI, that because EI consists of a range of skills and abilities, in a similar vein to the measurement of other skills, these skills can be measured!

In other words, yes, EI ability tests are legitimate measures of EI.

What's in an Emotional Intelligence Questionnaire?

To show what to expect from an EI □uestionnaire, I will now provide an example of an EI-□uiz (Mind Tools, 2019). In this quiz, 15 statements are presented and responders are asked to answer as to how they really are, rather than how they think they should be:

I can recognize my emotions as I experience them

I lose my temper when I feel frustrated

People have told me that I'm a good listener

I know how to calm myself down when I feel anxious or upset

I enjoy organizing groups

I find it hard to focus on something over the long term

I find it difficult to move on when I feel frustrated or unhappy

I know my strengths and weaknesses

I avoid conflict and negotiations

I feel that I don't enjoy my work

I ask people for feedback on what I do well, and how I can improve

I set long-term goals and review my progress regularly

I find it difficult to read other people's emotions

I struggle to build rapport with others

I use active listening skills when people speak to me

For each of these statements, the responders would rate themselves from not at all, rarely, sometimes, often and very often (Mind Tools, 2019).

How is EI Measured?

Generally speaking, EI is measured in three different ways:

Self-report

Other-report

Ability measures

A variety of scales, quizzes and questionnaires have been developed for each of these methods of measuring EI. There are four general types of EI tests, which are described in more detail soon!

Abilities based tests (including the MSCEIT)

Trait-based tests (such as the Bar-On EQi)

Competency-based tests – (including the ESCI)

Behavior-based tests – (for example, the Genos)

Whilst all provide measures of EI, for situations where an accurate, objective assessment of EI is wanted (such as recruitment) the consensus from the research is to use the MSCEIT (Bradberry, 2014).

The Emotional Intelligence Scale

Schutte and colleagues (1998) developed a measure of emotional intelligence based on the model that was published by Salovey and Mayer in 1990. Sixty-two items were found to be reflective of the dimensions of Salovey and Mayer's model (Schutte, Malouff, Hall, Haggerty, Cooper, Golden, & Dornheim, 1998).

Then, a factor analysis of results from a study of 346 participants lead to the development of this 33-item scale:

I know when to speak about my personal problems to others

When I am faced with obstacles, I remember times I faced similar obstacles and overcame them

I expect that I will do well on most things I try

Other people find it easy to confide in me

I find it hard to understand the non-verbal messages of other people*

Some of the major events of my life have led me to re-evaluate what is important and not important

When my mood changes, I see new possibilities

Emotions are one of the things that make my life worth living

I am aware of my emotions as I experience them

I expect good things to happen

I like to share my emotions with others

When I experience a positive emotion, I know how to make it last

I arrange events others enjoy

I seek out activities that make me happy

I am aware of the non-verbal messages I send to others

I present myself in a way that makes a good impression on others

When I am in a positive mood, solving problems is easy for me

By looking at their facial expressions, I recognize the emotions people are experiencing

I know why my emotions change

When I am in a positive mood, I am able to come up with new ideas

I have control over my emotions

I easily recognize my emotions as I experience them

I motivate myself by imagining a good outcome to tasks I take on

I compliment others when they have done something well

I am aware of the non-verbal messages other people send

When another person tells me about an important event in his or her life, I almost feel as though I have experienced this event myself

When I feel a change in emotions, I tend to come up with new ideas

When I am faced with a challenge, I give up because I believe I will fail*

I know what other people are feeling just by looking at them

I help other people feel better when they are down

I use good moods to help myself keep trying in the face of obstacles

I can tell how people are feeling by listening to the tone of their voice

It is difficult for me to understand why people feel the way they do*

Further studies of this 33 – item measure found it to have good internal consistency and test-retest reliability.

4 Example Emotional Intelligence Tests and Questions

Are you now curious about EI tests? Perhaps the following description of four examples of EI tests can capture your interest!

1. The Emotional Quotient Inventory 2.0 (EQ-i-2.0)

This test was the first scientifically validated, and now the most extensively used, EI assessment worldwide (Australian Council for Educational Research, 2016).

It was developed from 20 years of global research. The EQ-i is a self-report measure for individuals aged 16 years and older and can be delivered online. It takes approximately 30 minutes, and participants are re□uired to respond to □uestions designed to assess key aspects of emotional skills related to life and workplace performance.

Such skills have been shown to affect performance in complex areas such as conflict resolution and planning (ACER, 2016).

The results from the EQ-i can provide respondents with information about emotional skills they can improve as well as those areas that they excel in – which can then lead to individuals having the capacity to utilize their strengths to maximize performance in daily tasks (ACER, 2016).

The EQ-i 2.0 is administered from an online portal that achieves simple and efficient administration, scoring and reporting.

Once an individual completes the test, a report is produced that takes the form of an inventory. The inventory includes 15 competencies that center around 5 composite areas of EI – self-perception, self-expression, interpersonal, decision-making and stress management (ACER, 2016).

Although taking the test is free, in order to administer the test a practitioner must meet the requirements of the EQ-i ☐ualification level.

The EQ-i is based on Bar-On's model of emotional-social intelligence, and it is accompanied by the EQ-360 (Consortium for Research on Emotional Intelligence in Organizations – CREIO, 2018).

The EQ-360 provides a more comprehensive analysis of EQ because it also includes information provided by others. Observer ratings are then considered in conjunction with the results of an EQ-i-2.0 self-report to give a more detailed profile (CREIO, 2018).

2. Profile of Emotional Competence (PEC)

This test was developed by Brasseur & Mikolajczak and provides separate measures of intra-personal EI and inter-personal EI (CREIO, 2018). It looks at 5 core emotional competencies – identification, understanding, expression, regulation, and use of emotions – in the self and others.

It has been extensively validated in research, with results taken from a total sample of almost 22 000 individuals (CREIO, 2018). It is available free of charge for research and clinical purposes.

The full PEC consists of 50 items and takes approximately 1-15 minutes to administer, and the short form includes 20 items and takes 5 – 10 minutes to complete. The PEC is a self-report measure, however, it needs to be administered by a psychologist who is familiar with the emotional intelligence and emotional competence research and theory (CREIO, 2018).

3. The Trait Emotional Intelligence Questionnaire (TEIQue)

The TEIQue was developed by Dr. K. V. Petrides and is available free of charge for academic and clinical research (CREIO, 2018).

The full-form consists of 153 items, measuring 15 distinct facets, 4 factors and global trait EI. The short-form is a 30-item test that measures global trait EI which was developed from the full-form TEIQue (CREIO, 2018).

Based on correlations with corresponding total facet scores, 2 items were selected for inclusion from each of the 15 facets of the full-form TEIQue.

This questionnaire is also presented to gather ratings from observers – the TEIQue 360° and 360° Short-form (CREIO, 2018). Dr. Stella Mavroveli also designed the TEIQue Child-form that is suited to children aged 8 – 12 years.

This questionnaire consists of 75 items which are responded to on a 5-point scale and looks at the nine distinct facets of trait EI in children (CREIO, 2018).

4. Wong's Emotional Intelligence Scale (WEIS)

This is a self-report measure of EI designed to be used by Chinese respondents (CREIO, 2018). It is based on the four ability dimensions mentioned previously that make up EI. It consists of two parts:

The first part includes 20 scenarios. Respondents choose the option that most closely reflects the reaction they are likely to have in each scenario that is described (CREIO, 2018)

The second part is made up of 20 ability pairs. Respondents are required to select one of two types of abilities that best demonstrates their strength (CREIO, 2018).

Now that we have looked at EI tests, let's consider the types of questions that appear in these assessments. The following questions, from the PEC (Profile of Emotional Competence), are similar to those used in a variety of EI tests.

Hopefully they can provide you with an idea of what it may be like to do an EQ test!

Sample Questions (accessed from CREIO, 2018):

As my emotions arise I don't know where they came from

I don't always understand why I respond in the way I do

If I wanted, I could easily influence other people's emotions to achieve what I want

I know what to do to win people over to my cause

When I feel good, I can easily tell whether it is due to being proud of myself, happy or relaxed

I am good at describing my feelings

I can easily get what I want from others

I easily manage to calm myself down after a difficult experience

Most of the time I understand why people feel the way they do

When I am sad, I find it easy to cheer myself up

I find it difficult to handle my emotions

When I am angry, I find it easy to calm myself down

I am often surprised by people's responses because I was not aware they were in a bad mood

My feelings help me to focus on what is important to me

Others don't accept the way I express my emotions

When I am sad, I often don't know why

In a stressful situation I usually think in a way that helps me stay calm

Are There 'Right Answers' to EQ Assessments?

In fact, yes, there are so-called 'right answers' to EQ assessments – however, this only applies to the objective measures of EQ… obviously, there is no such thing as a 'correct' answer in a self-report assessment!

Research has included efficacious ways to identify 'correct' alternatives in EQ tests– e.g. in facial perception, or meanings of emotions terms (Mayer et al., 2003). This has been claimed due to the convergence between expert and general consensus on EI measures (Mayer et al., 2003). So-called 'right answers' are based on criteria developed from research (Mayer et al., 2003).

What Does an EQ Score Mean?

EQ is an emotional quotient score. It is found by assessing the behavioral factors that reflect EI. For example, the EQ score reflects the way in which a person reacts in a variety of situations, including:

Stressful or frustrating situations

Failures, or disappointing situations

Positions of leadership

How an individual manages the emotions of people of a range of different ages, and

Handling diversity and cultural sensitivities (My Frameworks, 2017).

EQ distinguishes emotional capacity as a distinct type of intellect. The average EQ score is in the range of 90 – 100, whilst the perfect EQ score is 160. What does an EQ score actually mean? Well, as well as contributing to success, EQ plays a role in everyday life (My Frameworks, 2017).

Six EQ Self-assessments

Maybe you are interested in testing your own EQ? Listed below are 6 readily available EQ self-assessments:

Emotional Intelligence Test (2019). Psychology Today..

Test your E.I: Free EQ quiz (2018). Institute for Health and Human Potential.

How Emotionally Intelligent are You? Boosting Your People Skills (2019). Mind Tools.

Emotional Intelligence Test (2019). Psych Tests.

Emotional Intelligence Test Free – EQ Test Free Online (2019). Alpha High IQ Society.

How Emotionally Intelligent Are You? (2017). My Frameworks.

MEASURING EMOTIONAL INTELLIGENCE IN THE WORKPLACE

EI is closely associated with success in the workplace (Bradberry, 2014).

TalentSmart, a worldwide leader in the provision of emotional intelligence, examined EI alongside 33 other key workplace skills. It was discovered that EI was, in this case, the strongest predictor of performance (Bradberry, 2014). Actually, EI explained 58% of success in all job types!

How, then, is EI measured in the workplace?

The Consortium for Research on Emotional Intelligence in Organizations (CREIO) have reviewed a number of tests that promise to measure EI in workplace settings, and have selected those for which there is a substantial body of research. Let's examine these different measures.

The Emotional and Social Competence Inventory (ESCI)

This is used to measure EI and enables workplaces to raise awareness of EI based on feedback (CREIO, 2018).

A multi-rater assessment, this test also encourages the coaching and development of crucial work capabilities. It takes approximately 30 – 45 minutes to administer.

It looks at the following competency scales:

- ✓ Emotional self-awareness,
- ✓ Emotional self-control,
- ✓ Adaptability,
- ✓ Achievement orientation,
- ✓ Positive outlook,
- ✓ Empathy,
- ✓ Organizational awareness,
- ✓ Coach and mentor,
- ✓ Inspirational leadership,
- ✓ Influence,
- ✓ Conflict management and
- ✓ Teamwork (CREIO, 2018).

Is an EQ Test the Same as an Intelligence Test?

For many years, intelligence tests have been used to look at quantifying a person's cognitive ability – their capacity to reason and 'think'. However, EI is a relatively new concept. Hopefully, this article has shown that EI (or 'EQ') can be measured, so, can an EQ test be compared to an IQ test?

There is a key, crucial difference between testing EQ versus testing IQ. Notably, IQ (the intelligence □uotient) measures, broadly speaking, the ability to learn. It is stable, changing very little across the lifespan. On the other hand, the emotional □uotient (EQ) taps into EI – which is a flexible group of skills.

Therefore, like all skills, EI can be learned/acquired. It can be improved with practice.

In other words, it is possible to develop a high EI even if a person is not necessarily 'born with it'. As has been argued in this article, the 'ability' of EI can be measured…therefore, the closest comparison between tests of EQ and so-called 'intelligence tests' (such as the Wechsler tests and more recently, the Woodcock-Johnson test) is an abilities-based emotional intelligence test such as the MSCEIT.

Abilities-based EQ tests, such as the MEIS and the MSCEIT assess the actual emotional 'ability' of a person, in the same way that an IQ test measures cognitive ability.

Therefore, whilst not ALL EQ tests are the same as an intelligence test, abilities-based EI assessments share similar properties to IQ tests.

The issue of emotional intelligence testing is a really complicated one. Although not all tests of EI can be compared to IQ tests, hopefully this article has explained that EQ is a construct that can be measured. Emotional intelligence is a relatively new area of positive psychology, so expect to hear more about it as time goes on!

Chapter Eight

HOW TO DEVELOP EMOTIONAL INTELLIGENCE: 5 POWERFUL SECRETS

An astronaut is probably the most difficult job to land on the planet. Of tens of thousands of applications, NASA selects roughly half a dozen each decade. The application process is rigorous and highly demanding. You have to be a total badass to ☐ualify. You have to have deep expertise in science and engineering. You need at least 1,000 hours of piloting experience. You have to be physically fit and strong. And, most of all, you have to be a smart motherfucker.

Lisa Nowak was all of these things. She had a master's degree in aeronautical engineering and had studied postgraduate astrophysics at the U.S. Naval Academy. She flew air missions for the U.S. Navy in the Pacific for over five years. And in 1996, she was one of the fortunate few to be selected to become an astronaut.

Clearly, she was smart as hell. But in 2007, after discovering that her lover was seeing another woman, Lisa drove 15 hours straight, in a diaper, from Houston to Orlando, in order to confront her boyfriend's new s☐ueeze in an airport parking lot. Lisa packed zip ties, pepper spray, and large garbage bags and had some vague-but-not-really-thought-through plan to kidnap the woman. But before she could even get the woman out of her car, Lisa had an emotional breakdown, resulting in her ☐uickly being arrested.

Emotional intelligence is a concept researchers came up with in the 1980s and 90s to explain why intelligent people like Lisa often do really, really stupid things. The argument went that the same way your general intelligence (IQ) is a measurement of your ability to process information and come to sound decisions, your emotional intelligence (EQ) is your ability to process emotions—both others' and your own—and come to sound decisions.

Some people have an incredibly high IQ but low EQ—think your nutty professor who can't match his socks or doesn't see the purpose in showering. Other people have incredibly high EQ but low IQ—think the street hustler who can't even spell his own name but somehow talks you into giving him the shirt off your back.

Psychologists who study emotional intelligence sometimes claim that it is actually more important than general intelligence. This statement is controversial at best, and a big bag o' "what the fuck?" at worst. For one, measuring emotional intelligence is difficult, if not impossible. Most of this stuff is subjective.

But also because emotional intelligence isn't as stable as general intelligence is. IQ is harder to change. But EQ is something you can work on and develop like a muscle or a skill and watch grow, like a dainty flower in your stupid ass garden.

So, basically, no matter how smart you are, you have no excuse. Get your shit together. Developing emotional intelligence comes down to not being a fucknut like Lisa was.

Here Are Five Ways To Start Doing It.

1) Self-Awareness

This one is first and that's not random. Self-awareness is the most essential of emotional intelligence skills. Why?

Because without this guy you've got no way to evaluate what skills you have, what you lack and what you need to work on. You're flying blind. So what's the formal definition?

Self-awareness means having a deep understanding of one's emotions, strengths, weaknesses, needs, and drives. People with strong self-awareness are neither overly critical nor unrealistically hopeful. Rather, they are honest with themselves and with others. People who have a high degree of self-awareness recognize how their feelings affect them, other people, and their job performance.

Want to know the best shortcut for identifying if someone is high in self-awareness or not?

One of the hallmarks of self-awareness is a self-deprecating sense of humor.

To make fun of yourself — and get a laugh — you have to know yourself and how you are perceived.

So how do you increase self-awareness? Get feedback. You don't always see yourself accurately. And this friend or that friend doesn't always see you accurately. But if you survey five or ten pals, you're going see some very accurate trends.

From Insight:

…other people generally see us more objectively than we see ourselves. Psychologist Timothy Smith and his colleagues powerfully demonstrated this in a study with 300 married couples in which both partners were being tested for heart disease. They asked each participant to rate both their own and their partner's levels of anger, hostility, and argumentativeness- all strong predictors of the illness- and found that people's self-ratings were infinitely less accurate than those of their spouses. Another study asked more than 150 Navy officers and their subordinates to rate the officers' leadership style, and found that only the subordinates could accurately assess their bosses' performance and promotability.

So you see yourself more accurately. That's great, but we all know someone who is aware they're a jerk — and yet keep acting like a jerk. So what do we need to complement our new self-knowledge?

2) Self-Regulation

I love when people say, "I'm very emotional. I must have very high emotional intelligence." Sorry, being very emotional doesn't make you high in EI; it just makes you a drama queen.

However, being able to regulate your emotions is a big part of EI. People who are wise and warm don't impulsively respond to things or act without thinking.

Biological impulses drive our emotions. We cannot do away with them — but we can do much to manage them. Self-regulation, which is like an ongoing inner conversation, is the component of emotional intelligence that frees us from being prisoners of our feelings. People engaged in such a conversation feel bad moods and emotional impulses just as everyone else does, but they find ways to control them and even to channel them in useful ways.

People who can self-regulate make better decisions, are more resilient, and act with more integrity. (They also tend not to eat an entire box of donuts in one sitting while obsessively checking Instagram, but this finding has yet to be supported by the literature.)

Mindfulness is an excellent, science-backed way to self-regulate. And while a full explanation of it is way beyond the scope of this post (you can get more info here) a little "mini-meditation" can be a big help.

Next time you feel your emotions surging, turn your attention to your breath. Focus on it going in and out. When your mind wanders, return your attention to your breath. Give it 10-20 seconds at first.

Neuroscience says even a little bit can calm those feelings and get your head on straight.

As these stressful thoughts were presented, the patients used either of two different attention stances: mindful awareness of their breath or distraction by doing mental arithmetic. Only mindfulness of their breath both lowered activity in the amygdala— mainly via a faster recovery— and strengthened it in the brain's attention networks, while the patients reported less stress reactivity.

So you know yourself and you can control yourself. But what EI component allows us to actually accomplish something with all that personal power?

3) Motivation

Yup, motivation is a part of EI. But we need to put a spin on the definition. Chasing money or promotions isn't a sign of emotional intelligence. EI means having an intrinsic desire to achieve and accomplish things.

Plenty of people are motivated by external factors, such as a big salary or the status that comes from having an impressive title or being part of a prestigious company. By contrast, those with leadership potential are motivated by a deeply embedded desire to achieve for the sake of achievement.

So how do we boost motivation? Track your accomplishments. Teresa Amabile's research at Harvard found that the single most motivating thing is progress in meaningful work. So when you move the needle forward, take note.

This pattern is what we call the progress principle: of all the positive events that influence inner work life, the single most powerful is progress in meaningful work; of all the negative events, the single most powerful is the opposite of progress— setbacks in the work.

Keep a list of everything you've accomplished today where you can see it. When I spoke to bestselling author Josh Kaufman, he said a "did-it" list is one of his primary productivity tools.

So the first three parts of emotional intelligence are about self-management. The next two are about how to deal with others. So where do we start?

4) Empathy

You're familiar with the word — but this one is actually a bit tricky.

The ability to understand the emotional makeup of other people. Skill in treating people according to their emotional reactions.

So why is it tricky? Because it's a balance. Too little — or too much — can cause problems.

Those whose sympathetic feelings become too strong may themselves suffer. In the helping professions, this can lead to compassion fatigue; in executives, it can create distracting feelings of anxiety about people and circumstances that are beyond anyone's control. But those who protect themselves by deadening their feelings may lose touch with empathy.

Don't worry; there's a solution. The research says there are actually three distinct types of empathy:

Emotional empathy: "You feel awful? Then I feel awful too!"

Cognitive empathy: "I understand that you are feeling awful. That must suck."

Compassion: "You feel awful? I feel for you. How can I help?"

All three have their place. You want friends and family to have emotional empathy. You want someone to really feel what you feel when you're down or to be thrilled with you when you're up.

However you don't want your surgeon crying so hard about your tumor that they can't perform the operation. You want them to have cognitive empathy.

And we can all do better with more compassion. With compassion we feel for, not with. And this drives us to want to help, while not emotionally impairing us from helping. Compassion is what we want to focus on for EI.

So how do you increase it? By using "Loving-Kindness Meditation." Yes, with a name like that you'd expect it to be taught to you by woodland fairies. Relax. Research by Emma Seppala at Stanford shows it works.

The best instructions I've found (that have no scientific jargon or mentions of elves) come from 10% Happier, the excellent book by Dan Harris:

1. This practice involves picturing a series of people and sending them good vibes. Start with yourself. Generate as clear a mental image as possible.

2. Repeat the following phrases: May you be happy, May you be healthy, May you be safe, May you live with ease. Do this slowly. Let the sentiment land. You are not forcing your well-wishes on anyone; you're just offering them up, just as you would a cool drink. Also, success is not measured by whether you generate any specific emotion. As Sharon says, you don't need to feel "a surge of sentimental love accompanied by chirping birds." The point is to try. Every time you do, you are exercising your compassion muscle. (By the way, if you don't like the phrases above, you can make up your own.)

3. After you've sent the phrases to yourself, move on to: a benefactor (a teacher, mentor, relative), a close friend (can be a

pet, too), a neutral person (someone you see often but don't really ever notice), a difficult person, and, finally, "all beings."

Don't get too worried about details. It's not a magic spell and this isn't Hogwart's. You can customize it. The important thing is wishing others well and expanding that feeling from those you feel strongly about to a wider and wider circle of people.

Four out of five. Not bad at all. And number five actually assembles those prior four together to turn you into a Voltron of emotional intelligence...

5) Social Skill

Social skills mean the ability to build rapport and manage relationships — with a goal in mind.

That doesn't make it Machiavellian. Think of the concepts of "leadership" or "parenting." Both are relationships, but both also have a purpose greater than merely enjoying the other person's company.

Social skill, rather, is friendliness with a purpose: moving people in the direction you desire, whether that's agreement on a new marketing strategy or enthusiasm about a new product. Socially skilled people tend to have a wide circle of acquaintances, and they have a knack for finding common ground with people of all kinds-a knack for building rapport.

So how do you build EI social skills? Luckily, this one is easy. Seriously. Not that becoming socially adept is simple — it's actually quite complex.

But that said, if you have made big strides in the first four, this fifth component of EI tends to grow on its own without much effort.

Social skill is the culmination of the other dimensions of emotional intelligence. People tend to be very effective at managing relationships when they can understand and control their own emotions and can empathize with the feelings of others. Even motivation contributes to social skill. Remember that people who are driven to achieve tend to be optimistic, even in the face of setbacks or failure. When people are upbeat, their "glow" is cast upon conversations and other social encounters. They are popular, and for good reason. Because it is the outcome of the other dimensions of emotional intelligence, social skill is recognizable on the job in many ways that will by now sound familiar. Socially skilled people, for instance, are adept at managing teams-that's their empathy at work. Likewise, they are expert persuaders-a manifestation of self-awareness, self-regulation, and empathy combined.

(And if there are specific elements of social skills you want to work on: here's how to make friends, to get people to like you, to network, to read people, and how to be someone people love to talk to.)

So work on the first four components of EI and then spend more time with others, facing new challenges. Self-aware, self-regulated, motivated people with empathy mostly just need practice to build their social skills.

Alright, your EI burns so bright I'm gonna need sunscreen. Let's round it all up and learn the final critical point that will help you be more emotionally intelligent…

Sum Up

Here's how to increase emotional intelligence:

Self-awareness: "I should have posted this earlier in the week. When I'm really busy with super-important stuff or, um, when I see a cute puppy video on YouTube, I know blogging gets delayed."

Self-regulation: "You need to cool it with the puppy videos, Eric. Next time, we only watch the tiny Husky puppy howl like a little wolf once, and then we do a mini-meditation and get back to work. Seriously."

Motivation: "I have an Excel spreadsheet of puppy videos watched, mini-meditations done, and how often the blog posts have been completed on time. More posting, more meditating, fewer howling, insanely cute puppies."

Empathy: "I'm not going to beat myself up about this. The post still got done. I'm happy with it. And that puppy video was really cute. I'm showing some self-compassion here. Also, I'm including the puppy in my Loving-Kindness Meditation today. May the little guy live with ease."

Social skills: "Enough about me and my addiction; how are you?"

So what's the final thing you need to know about EI?

Balance. We need to work on all of the skills and then we need to make sure they work together. Does this sound like I made a hard process even harder? Don't worry.

You don't need to score 100% in any component. In fact, you don't want to. Like I said, too much empathy can be a problem. It can lead to emotional fatigue. By the same token, John Mayer, one of the originators of EI, says too much self-awareness can even be a problem.

In fact, too much self-awareness can reduce self-esteem, which is often a crucial component of great leadership.

So improve all the components and then focus on finding the balance between them that works for you. You don't need to be perfect at any one of them. The symphony is more about how the musicians play together than how great any one of them is.

Knowing yourself, controlling yourself and motivating yourself. Feeling for others and having the skills to connect with them. This is what allows you to accomplish great things at work and to give your loved ones what they need.

Lisa Nowak, for all of her brilliance and expertise, couldn't handle her own emotions and valued the wrong things. Therefore, she let her emotions drive her off the proverbial cliff, going from outer space to incarcerated space.

Ultimately, we're always choosing what we value, whether we know it or not. And our emotions will carry out those values through motivating our behavior in some way.

So in order to live the life you truly want to live, you have to first be clear about what you truly value because that's where your emotional energy will be directed.

And knowing what you truly value—not just what you say you value—is probably the most emotionally intelligent skill you can develop.

CONCLUSION

Successfully relating to people re☐uires being able to read and understand their feelings and what motivates them. Understanding yourself and others is essential to build the emotional resonance necessary to achieve ambitious goals in business and personal relationships. Start now!

Famous College Dropouts: include Reggie Jackson, Steve Jobs, Ben Affleck, Woody Allen, Hans Christian Anderson, Dan Ackroyd, Kate Beckinsale, James Cameron, and Mark Zuckerberg (founder of Facebook and the world's youngest self-made millionaire).

Famous People Who Have Failed (but had great emotional intelligence.)

1. He was fired from a newspaper for his lack of imagination and original ideas - Walt Disney.

2. She was dismissed from acting school with a note that said she was too shy - Lucille Ball.

3. He was a failed soldier, farmer and real estate agent who at 38-years-old went to work for his father as a handyman - Ulysses S. Grant.

4. He was cut from his high school basketball team, went home, locked himself in his room and cried - Michael Jordan.

5. He failed in business twice, had a nervous breakdown and was defeated in eight elections - Abraham Lincoln.

6. His teacher told him he was too stupid to learn anything and that he should go into a field that emphasized his pleasant personality - Thomas Edison.

7. They were turned down by a recording company and told guitar music was on the way out - the Beatles.

Today, emotional intelligence is a key to success in life and the good news is that whatever your actual level of emotional intelligence, you can improve it The best way to develop your emotional skills is through practice. You can then become more efficient at recognizing and managing your emotions as well as the emotions of others and lead a happier, more successful and fulfilled life. Always remember the wise words of Daniel Goleman who said, "What really matters for success, character, happiness and lifelong achievements is a definite set of emotional skills - your EQ - not just purely cognitive abilities that are measured by conventional IQ tests."

Do Not Go Yet; One Last Thing To Do

If you enjoyed this book or found it useful I'd be very grateful if you'd post a short review on Amazon. Your support really does make a difference and I read all the reviews personally so I can get your feedback and make this book even better.

Thanks again for your support!

www.ingramcontent.com/pod-product-compliance
Lightning Source LLC
Chambersburg PA
CBHW020318290526
45785CB00007B/2834